Choosing to Teach, Choosing to See

Choosing to Teach, Choosing to See

Critical Readings for Those Entering the Noble Profession of Education

First Edition

Edited by Ty-Ron M. O. Douglas and Ransford Pinto

SAN DIEGO

Bassim Hamadeh, CEO and Publisher
Angela Schultz, Senior Field Acquisitions Editor
Alisa Muñoz, Project Editor
Christian Berk, Production Editor
Emely Villavicencio, Senior Graphic Designer
Alexa Lucido, Licensing Manager
Natalie Piccotti, Director of Marketing
Kassie Graves, Vice President of Editorial
Jamie Giganti, Director of Academic Publishing

Copyright © 2021 by Cognella, Inc. All rights reserved. No part of this publication may be reprinted, reproduced, transmitted, or utilized in any form or by any electronic, mechanical, or other means, now known or hereafter invented, including photocopying, microfilming, and recording, or in any information retrieval system without the written permission of Cognella, Inc. For inquiries regarding permissions, translations, foreign rights, audio rights, and any other forms of reproduction, please contact the Cognella Licensing Department at rights@cognella.com.

Trademark Notice: Product or corporate names may be trademarks or registered trademarks and are used only for identification and explanation without intent to infringe.

Cover image copyright © 2018 iStockphoto LP/fstop123.

Printed in the United States of America.

Contents

Introduction   vii

Reading 1A   Camaraderie: Reality and the Neoindigenous   1
Christopher Emdin

Reading 1B   Courage: Teach without Fear   13
Christopher Emdin

Reading 2   Teaching   23
Chris Mercagliano

Reading 3   Building a Caring Classroom That Supports Achievement   31

Reading 4   What's Radical Love Got to Do with It: Navigating Identity, Pedagogy, and Positionality in Pre-Service Education   77
Ty-Ron M. O. Douglas and Christine Nganga

Reading 5   White Privilege: Unpacking the Invisible Knapsack   101
Peggy McIntosh

Reading 6   Education by Any Means Necessary: Peoples of African Descent and Community-Based Pedagogical Spaces   107
Ty-Ron M. O. Douglas and Craig Peck

Reading 7   A Conversation on the Literacy Development of Urban Poor Youth: Perspectives from the Classroom, Neighborhood and University   135
Ty-Ron M. O. Douglas, James F. Baumann, Adrian C. Clifton, Lenny Sánchez, Veda McClain, Pamela Ingram, and Ellis A. Ingram

Introduction

Ty-Ron M. O. Douglas and Ransford Pinto

> *"To see what is in front of one's nose*
> *needs a constant struggle."*
> —George Orwell

I (TY-RON DOUGLAS) REMEMBER PREPARING FOR MY first day as a middle and high school English teacher like it was yesterday. Upon my arrival on campus, I was given a room key, a textbook, and a schedule. Enthusiastic yet cautious, I remember wondering, "But what am I supposed to teach exactly?" There was no specific curriculum guide and very little guidance. What I did have, however, was faith, confidence in my calling to the *noblest of professions*, and the capacity to help students ask critical questions of themselves and society. The questions I asked and continue to ask of my students are questions I ask myself to this very day. For example, "Who decides who gets to live well?" and "How would my life and educational journey have been different if I had been born and raised in Ferguson, Missouri, with the paternal side of my family rather than on the island of Bermuda?" These questions, particularly when considered within the context of the tragic death of Michael Brown, remind us that dynamics such as gender, social class, culture, race, place, and space matter systematically, systemically, and in the individual lives, identities, and outcomes of those we serve and teach. Certainly, how these dynamics impact and intersect with reform efforts, standards, curriculum and accountability inside and outside the schoolhouse must be seriously considered by educational stakeholders.

My (Ransford Pinto) commitment and experiences in teaching began in the classrooms of Ghana, West Africa where I taught middle social studies and math. I believe that the heart of teaching is relationship, and a foundation for establishing a trusting student–teacher relationship is the teacher knowing the names of his, her, or their students. So I started learning the names of my students from the first day of class. Through this experience, I have learned that a great student–teacher relationship enhances students' sense of belonging and self-confidence, which are positively correlated with higher academic achievement. Since that time, I have been privileged to engage in education in the United Kingdom and the United States. Across my global experiences, I have become acutely aware that there are effective teachers and there are those who are less so. Specific qualities of effective teachers include empathy, dynamism, reflection, care, and advocacy for students while maintaining high expectations for their academic and social performances. In my classes, I incorporate and value the experiences and views of all students. I approach teaching using postmodern epistemological guidance with a focus on creating an intellectually diverse and social environment wherein students and I engage in a mutually beneficial educational experience. I consider my role as a facilitator of learning and growth rather than the expert imparting knowledge. In my experiences as an instructor of preservice teachers, it is often evident which individuals possess the commitment and qualities to develop these skillsets. Hence, I challenge my students to reflect on questions like the following: Do I want to be an effective teacher? What are my assumptions about teaching and learning? What are my assumptions about students, families, and schools? How will I build bridges between myself and my students? Ultimately, effective teachers are those who honor the worth and dignity of their students and the noble profession.

To the core, we (Ty-Ron and Ransford) are educators. We love to teach! We teach with passion, conviction, and enthusiasm, and we teach and learn everywhere we go. As such, it wouldn't surprise you to know that we believe that teachers matter, and excellent teachers are often the difference makers in the lives of young people. Hopefully, if you are reading this edited volume, it is because you desire to be an excellent educator. In the pages of this book, you will encounter readings that will likely stretch you and perspectives that may differ from your personal views. This is both normal and expected for you as a reader and for us as editors and educators who are committed to your growth. In fact, the selection of these readings does not mean we agree with every statement or ideology espoused. Instead, these readings support the imperative that effective educators consider varying perspectives, evaluate the taken for granted, (re)consider our blind spots, and—in the words of Orwell—"see what is in front of [our] nose[s]."

The readings will invite you to hear, see, and consider the perspectives of others. The readings will ask you to reflect on where and how education takes place and for whom. The readings will challenge you to embrace the reality that the schoolhouse does not have a monopoly on education; instead, education, educators, and leaders exist in various spaces, and it is our responsibility as *excellent educators in preparation* not just to accept this reality but to leverage it for maximum educational impact! As editors, we've sought to include a multitude of diverse voices and ideologies that we believe will help us *see* students with an antideficit lens and filter what we see in society and in our classrooms more critically and comprehensively. The challenge for you is not just to think critically, but to read against the grain and to *go* on the journey of reflective exploration for yourself and your students. Ultimately, while it is true that teachers matter, our roles as teachers only matter because students matter most!

> *"The proposition that a true teacher is a fully holistic model*
> *and not merely a taskmaster or a classroom manager*
> *means it is impossible for teachers to lead their students*
> *any farther than they have already taken themselves."*
> —Chris Mercagliano

Reading 1A

Camaraderie
Reality and the Neoindigenous

Christopher Emdin

> *I am a man of substance, of flesh and bone, fiber and liquids—and I might even be said to possess a mind. I am invisible, understand, simply because people refuse to see me. Like the bodiless heads you see sometimes in circus sideshows, it is as though I have been surrounded by mirrors of hard, distorting glass. When they approach me they see only my surroundings, themselves, or figments of their imagination—indeed, everything and anything except me.*
> —Ralph Ellison

RALPH ELLISON'S *INVISIBLE MAN* DESCRIBES THE complexities of blackness in America and captures the ways that the segregated South and its ugly history of racism had inscribed itself so indelibly into the psyche of the "more accepting" and progressive North in the 1950s that it rendered African Americans invisible. The book's protagonist is so shaped by the conditions of his time that he becomes a distorted version of himself, his "true self" rendered invisible. This haunting and powerful story resonates with the experiences of urban youth in today's urban classrooms. The poet Adrienne Rich affirmed this sense of negation when she observed that "when someone with the authority of a teacher, say, describes the world and you are not in it, there is a moment of psychic disequilibrium, as if you looked in the mirror and saw nothing."[1]

Consider a common scenario in urban schools, and one I have witnessed often, where the teacher and student have different conceptions about what it means to be on time and prepared for class. For many students, being on time and

Christopher Emdin, "Camaraderie: Reality and the Neoindigenous," *For White Folks Who Teach in the Hood...and the Rest of Y'all Too*, pp. 17-30, 212. Copyright © 2016 by Beacon Press. Reprinted with permission.

prepared means being in or around the physical space of the classroom at the appointed hour and being able to access whatever materials are necessary for the day's instruction. This runs counter to a more narrowly defined, traditional perception of being prepared for learning, and can result in students being made invisible to the teacher. I experienced a perfect example of this "making invisible" process during a pre-suspension meeting for a student whose science teacher had accused her of being disruptive, unprepared for class, and habitually tardy. As the teacher began to describe the reasons for the suspension, the student stood up and said, "That's not true, that's just not true." Calmly, the principal asked the student to stop being disrespectful. The student looked bewildered and sat down with tears streaming down her face, biting at her thumb, her knee shaking so forcefully I thought she might knock the principal's desk over. At the end of the meeting, she snatched the pink sheet of paper that described the procedures for her two-day suspension and stormed out of the office. Her teacher seemed frozen to her seat as the scenario played out, unsure of what to do next.

A few minutes later, having heard the teacher's litany of complaints that had led to the student's suspension, I walked through the school building and spotted the student in the middle of a crowd of friends. They had rallied around her and seemed to be consoling her. When I asked her if we could talk, she looked up reluctantly and slowly walked toward me. As she did so, a bell rang signaling the change of classroom periods. The students who had gathered around their friend quickly dispersed, heading to their respective classrooms. I noticed that a significant number of them stood at the doors of the classrooms or lingered between the doorways, shouting greetings to their friends who were passing by. As we walked the hallway, she pointed to a friend who pointed back at her, then asked me, "Is *he* late? Is *he* unprepared for class?" She then motioned to another friend who was straddling the doorway to a class and asked, "Is *she* late? Is *she* distracting the class?" I didn't quite know how to respond and so I didn't. She took that to mean that I understood her. "Exactly," she said. "I'm always ready for that lady's class and she gets me suspended because she doesn't know what she's doing. She sees what she wants to see." As we talked more, I mentioned that the teacher said she never had her books with her for class. She responded that a friend shares her books with her and lends her something to write with whenever she needs it. For her, that made it obvious that she was prepared to learn. She then mentioned that she was always on time for class. "I'm always at the door when that bell rings. I'm always there." The student saw herself as prepared and on time, but the teacher did not see the student the way she saw herself.

The point here is not to debate whether the teacher or the student was right or wrong; there isn't a clear answer to that question. What's important to note is that the teacher in this scenario had rendered the student's self-image as "prepared and on time" invisible. That image had been replaced with one in which the student was seen as disruptive, chronically late, and unprepared, a distortion of the student's self-image. This was the case even though the student mentioned that she liked the subject being taught and was excited about what she was learning in her science class. This teacher, who struggled to get her students engaged in science, had alienated one of the few students who liked the class, because she did not fit the mold the school and the teacher had cast for what a good student looks and acts like.

==The reality is that we privilege people who look and act like us, and perceive those who don't as different and, frequently, inferior.== In urban schools, and especially for those who haven't had previous experience in urban contexts or with youth of color, educators learn "best practices" from "experts" in the field, deemed as such because they have degrees, write articles, and meet other criteria that do not have anything to do with their work within urban communities. In fact, many of us who think about the education of youth of color have developed our ideas about the field from specialists who can describe the broad landscape of urban education but are often far removed, both geographically and psychologically, from the schools and students that they speak and write about so eloquently.

Urban education experts typically don't live in urban communities. They don't look like the students they discuss in meetings and conferences, and when they do, they often make class distinctions that separate them from students. Most importantly, they don't consider their distance from these communities as an impediment to their ability to engage in the work within them. The leaders within the field of urban education can't fathom the day-to-day experiences of urban students who see themselves as ready to learn despite not being perceived that way. They don't see the deep connections that exist between urban experience and school performance; many more have come to view school as a discrete space, as if what happens outside school has little to no impact on what happens inside school. This discourse among "experts" (politicians, professors, media pundits) has made it okay for teachers to work within urban communities they either refuse to live in or are afraid to live in. The nature of how we view urban-education expertise has created a context that dismisses students' lives and experiences while concurrently speaking about, and advocating for, equity and improving schools. Consider, for example, the growing number of new charter schools in urban communities with words like *success, reform,* and *equity* in their names and mission statements, but which engage in teaching practices that focus on making the school and the students within it as separate from the community as possible.

I engaged in a Twitter debate with one of these educators recently and was astounded by the fervor with which he defended his school's practice of "cleaning these kids up and giving them a better life." With that statement, he described everything that is wrong with the culture of urban education and the biggest hindrance to white folks who teach in the hood. First, the belief that students are in need of "cleaning up" presumes that they are dirty. Second, the aim of "giving them a better life" indicates that their present life has little or no value. The idea that one individual or school can give students "a life" emanates from a problematic savior complex that results in making students, their varied experiences, their emotions, and the good in their communities invisible. So invisible, in fact, that the chief way to teach urban youth of color more effectively—that is, to truly be in and in touch with their communities—is not seen as a viable option.

Physical Place and Emotional Space

To be in touch with the community, one has to enter into the physical places where the students live, and work to be invited into the emotion-laden spaces the youth inhabit. The places may be housing projects or overcrowded apartment buildings, but the spaces are what philosopher Kelly Oliver describes as psychic.[2] They are filled with emotions like fear, anger, and a shared alienation from the norms of school, birthed from experiences both within and outside the school building. The places transcend geography and are more about what is felt by being in a particular location.

The urban youth who inhabit these complex psychic spaces, and for whom imagination is the chief escape from harsh realities, walk through life wrapped in a shroud of emotions whose fibers are their varied daily experiences. The gunshot that rang past an apartment window (the experience) and the fear and anxiety that resulted from it (the emotion) creates a reality that is almost impossible for an outsider to fully comprehend. I remember being a tenth-grade student who attended a large comprehensive "specialized" urban public school. I took the train for an hour each day because the school I attended was better than the local ones in my neighborhood. One evening after a long day and what seemed like an equally long train ride home, I walked into my apartment building, and just as the large metal door closed behind me gunshots rang out just outside the door. I froze for a second, not knowing where the shots were coming from, when my younger sister, tugging at my arm, pulled me through the interior door of our apartment building as the shots continued to ring behind me. When I got into my family's apartment that night, and my sister described what had happened to my mother, she told me that I couldn't afford to freeze up in moments like that. I was told to be alert and drop to the floor at the sound of gunfire.

About a week later, I sat in my mathematics class as the teacher droned on about how to solve an equation. The class was silent except for the scratching of chalk against the blackboard as the teacher worked on the problem. A chair held the door open to let air into the classroom, but it wasn't enough to alleviate the stifling atmosphere in the boring class. As the teacher continued to write, a loud noise suddenly erupted from out in the hallway. Before I could even think, I jumped out of my seat and underneath my desk. I cowered on the floor for what seemed like forever until I heard my entire class break out in roaring laughter. I emerged from underneath the desk to find my teacher standing in the aisle and another student admonishing me for trying to be the class clown. The teacher's left hand hit my desk with a light thud and his right one pointed toward the door as the words "Principal's office, now" rolled from his lips. The class continued laughing as I grabbed my books and headed toward the door. In that moment, I couldn't find the words to explain that the loud sound I had heard reminded me of the shootout that I had barely missed getting caught in a week ago. There was no way to describe that the trauma of my experience the previous week was what caused me to jump under the desk in fear for my life. There was no way that the teacher or the principal could ever understand what I was feeling in that moment unless they had experienced it, and so I coolly grabbed my jacket and books, put on a smile for my friends, winked at the teacher, and walked out of the classroom.

Much research has been done on post-traumatic stress disorder and its impact on those afflicted. We tend to associate PTSD with combat veterans, but too often we fail to recognize that young people experience trauma regularly in ways that go unnoticed or unrecognized. For example, a study I conducted with black males who had either attended or were presently enrolled in urban public schools revealed symptoms of PTSD among participants. My coresearcher on the project, PTSD specialist and psychologist Napoleon Wells, identified the students' avoidance of certain discussions and reactions to others as similar to the ways that veterans respond after exposure to trauma. In fact, the students' symptoms of fear, anger, and powerlessness led to what Dr. Wells calls postracial tension stress disorder, which derives from youth seeing themselves as powerless in a world that conveys to them the message that race doesn't matter, at the same time it subjects them to physical and symbolic violence (at the hands of police and schools) because of their race.

In schools, urban youth are expected to leave their day-to-day experiences and emotions at the door and assimilate into the culture of schools. This process of personal repression is in itself traumatic and directly impacts what happens in the classroom. Students exist in a space within the classroom while the teacher limits their understanding to what is happening in the classroom place. Failure to prepare teachers to appreciate the psychic spaces students occupy inevitably limits their effectiveness. Some teachers understand that students come from places beyond the classroom and can acknowledge that these places have an effect on students and the spaces they occupy. However, many teachers cannot see beyond their immediate location (the school) and therefore have a very limited understanding of space. Many more are taught to ignore psychic space altogether, and therefore cannot fathom what it must be like for students to whom the classroom is a breeding ground for traumatic experiences. Once again, these students are unseen by teachers, mere reflections of teachers' perceptions of who they are. This is what Ellison described as people not seeing him but "surroundings, themselves, or figments of their imagination—indeed, everything and anything except me."[3]

==The work to become truly effective educators in urban schools requires a new approach to teaching that embraces the complexity of place, space, and their collective impact on the psyche of urban youth.== This approach is necessary whether we are talking about pre-service educators about to embark on their first year of teaching, those who have been in the field for a while, or the millions of people who have been drawn into the dysfunctional web of urban education as a parent, policymaker, or concerned citizen. Addressing the issues that plague urban education requires a true vision that begins with seeing students in the same way they see themselves.

Urban youth are typically well aware of the loss, pain, and injustice they experience, but are ill equipped for helping each other through the work of navigating who they truly are and who they are expected to be in a particular place. At seventeen years old, Youth Poet Laureate of the City of Oakland, California, Obasi Davis wrote the poem "Bored in 1st Period." Obasi, who is now a college student in a predominantly white institution of higher education, wrote this piece as a high school student seeing peers who are rendered invisible by their school and teachers even as he could see their true selves in plain view. In the excerpts of the poem reprinted below, the reader can see his deep analysis of his peers and the difference between who they are in the classroom (place) and who they truly are within a shared emotional space.

> BORED IN 1ST PERIOD
> Asia comes from repossessed dreams and nightmares that last as long as the absence of her father
>   I think that's the reason her clothes are always so Boa
>   Constricting any amount of longing she might have felt for him to me
> Daniel spent his childhood running from Richmond bullets and the ghost of his dad
>   Daniel is a *thug*
> He brags about seeing grown men ground to dust under heavy boots for their iPhones and their wallets
>   He rocks a long gold chain, a grill, and two diamond
>   earrings with
>   every outfit
>   Daniel only cares about money
>   but I can see genius bursting from his pained skin
>   It is the deepest black, pure like Earth's blood
>   but for some reason, most seem to see it as an
>   *impurity.*
>   He paints himself a gangster to cover what they call ugly
>   Jonathan chooses to come to class once a month or whenever we have a sub

> He shoots dice in the back corner of the classroom with Duma
> and Daniel
> When I ask them why, they tell me money is everything.
> It seems they are the products of a broken society and a torn home
> My home is not broken
> My parents are divorced but they get along
> I haven't known death to come close,
> and violence hasn't found me vulnerable
> And then, while sitting in 1st period pretending to read Macbeth,
> it clicked for me
> My classmates and I are different
> In the words of Dr. King our elbows are together yet
> our hearts are
> apart
> I'm not asking for some all holy savior to come and coddle us
> into equality
> I'm asking for you to understand our struggles and our hardships
> ==To understand that if we have to learn with each other we should also learn about each other so we can bring each other up==

What Obasi describes in this poem is a reality that many who interact with students on a daily basis will never see. He describes students in a classroom (place) who exist in worlds/spaces wholly distinct from the classroom. He shows us that what educators and the world at large see when looking at students is often a distortion of their authentic selves. Furthermore, he alludes to the major premise of this work—that what lies beyond what we see are deep stories, complex connections, and realities that factors like race, class, power, and the beliefs/presuppositions educators hold inhibit them from seeing. ==Teaching to who students are requires a recognition of their realities.==

John Searle defines reality as an agreed-upon outlook on or about social life based on how it is perceived or created by a group of people. He also sees reality as "facts relative to a system of values that we hold."[4] This definition provides a simple yet necessary framework for understanding youth realities—because it moves educators to focus on the ways that youth see the world and their position in it based on the facts, laws, rules, and principles that govern the places they are from and the consequent spaces they inhabit. This provides the educator with a very different vantage point for seeing them and gives information about place while providing insight into emotional space.

In order to fully understand youth realities, and make some sense of the powerful connection between youth realities, place, and space, I argue that educators need a new lens and vocabulary. This is why I argue for making connections between urban youth, or the neoindigenous, and the indigenous. While the word *neoindigeneity* may appear to the reader as yet another loaded academic term that has no significance in real urban classrooms, it is far from that. I use this term throughout this work as a way to make sense of the realities of the urban youth experience. Framing urban youth as neoindigenous, and understanding that the urban youth experience is deeply connected to the indigenous experience, provides teachers with a very different worldview when working with youth. From this new vantage point, teachers can see, access, and utilize tools for teaching urban youth. An understanding of neoindigineity allows educators to go beyond what they physically see when working with urban youth, and attend to the relationship between place and space.

For the indigenous, the relationship to emotional space is a constitutive part of their existence. For these populations, when one is hurt, healing requires addressing both physical wounds and the "soul wounds." Healing the physical wound occurs in a certain place, but healing the soul wound requires being in a space. The psychologist Eduardo Duran states that counseling Native Americans and other indigenous people requires entering into the spaces in which they reside, because as Mark Findlay identifies, there are understandings that cannot be visible within the institutions (places) of the power wielder.[5] This type of healing work is necessary for the neoindigenous as well. Situations such as the suspension of the student who believed she was prepared for class and always on time result in soul wounds that are bigger than the disciplinary issue itself and could be avoided if the teacher validated the student's emotion by allowing her to articulate her feelings. Recognizing the neoindigeneity of youth requires acknowledgement of the soul wounds that teaching practices inflict upon them.

If we are truly interested in transforming schools and meeting the needs of urban youth of color who are the most disenfranchised within them, educators must create safe and trusting environments that are respectful of students' culture. Teaching the neoindigenous requires recognition of the spaces in which they reside, and an understanding of how to see, enter into, and draw from these spaces. [...]I [will] describe how educators may engage in this healing process through an approach to teaching I call reality pedagogy.

Reality Pedagogy

Reality pedagogy is an approach to teaching and learning that has a primary goal of meeting each student on his or her own cultural and emotional turf. It focuses on making the local experiences of the student visible and creating contexts where there is a role reversal of sorts that positions the student as the expert in his or her own teaching and learning, and the teacher as the learner. It posits that while the teacher is the person charged with delivering the content, the student is the person who shapes how best to teach that content. Together, the teacher and students co-construct the classroom space.

Reality pedagogy allows for youth to reveal how and where teaching and learning practices have wounded them. The approach works toward making students wholly visible to each other and to the teacher and focuses on open discourse about where students are academically, psychologically, and emotionally. In a reality-pedagogy-based classroom, every individual is perceived as having a distinct perspective and is given the opportunity to express that in the classroom. There is no grand narrative. Instead of seeing the students as equal to their cultural identity, a reality pedagogue sees students as individuals who are influenced by their cultural identity. This means that the teacher does not see his or her classroom as a group of African American, Latino, or poor students and therefore does not make assumptions about their interests based on those preconceptions. Instead, the teacher begins from an understanding of the students as unique individuals and then develops approaches to teaching and learning that work for those individuals. This approach acknowledges the preconceptions, guilt, and biases a white teacher in a predominantly African American or Latino urban school may bring to the classroom because it considers the history of teaching and learning in contexts like the Carlisle School and consciously avoids replicating them.

In preparing teachers to teach in urban schools, I often show still images of students from classroom videos that I have collected over the last decade. The students in the images range in age from six to twenty-one and are all students of color from urban schools across the country. Each image shows students in varying poses of what could be described as disinterest. They range from heads rested on classroom desks or on palms that seem to be holding up much more than weary heads to students looking at the teacher with blank, emotionless stares. In one exercise, these images were presented to the teachers in whose classrooms the pictures were taken, and the teachers were asked to describe the students' realities. I would ask teachers to look at the images and describe what was going through each student's mind at the moment when his or her picture was taken. The responses from the teachers were quite similar and along the lines of "He doesn't want to be there" and "She is bored or angry." After this process, I provided teachers with transcripts from interviews with the students photographed, in which the students described what they were thinking and feeling at the moment their images were captured. Once this happened, the huge gap between how students experienced the world and how teachers viewed this same world became evident.

In one scenario, during a professional-development session where a large number of teachers from an urban school district gathered on a cold November afternoon, two images of an African American young man from a classroom in one of their schools were projected onto a screen. In one image, he is staring emptily into space, and in the other, his head is resting on his desk. Responses from the group were immediate, and all described the young man in the photos as some variation of "disinterested" or "unmotivated." I then hit the button on my laptop that played the video of the moments before and after the two images were taken. In the video, the young man tries repeatedly to answer a question that the teacher had posed. He raises his hand, stares at the teacher to get his attention, and even yells out the answer after he is initially ignored. After multiple futile attempts to be recognized by the teacher, he puts his head down on the desk.

When I interviewed this student after I had seen the video, he revealed a deep desire to learn and an undeniable frustration with the fact that the structures in place in the classroom, like his seat being at the back of the class, the pace of the lesson being too slow, and the students not having the space to discuss the content with each other, wouldn't allow this desire to be met. He mentioned that he put his head on the desk in an attempt to control the anger and frustration that came from not being validated and not being taught well. He knew that if he responded angrily, he would be perceived as "mad for no reason" and probably "kicked out of the class or suspended like they usually do when you say something." In this scenario, the different ways that teachers experienced the student's reaction to the classroom highlights the need for understanding the authentic realities of young people. A conversation with the teacher about this video revealed that, according to the teacher, the student had to learn to control his excitement and had not shown that he was ready to learn. In this scenario both the teacher and the student are experiencing the same classroom in very different ways.

Addressing the tensions that come out of these two authentic yet very different realities requires an approach to teaching and learning that functions to bridge the differences in experience within the classroom while allowing the teacher and student to co-construct a learning space that meets their unique needs. Reality pedagogy focuses on privileging the ways that students make sense of the classroom while acknowledging that the teacher often has very different expectations about the classroom. This approach to teaching focuses on the subtleties of teaching and learning that are traditionally glossed over by teachers and administrators while addressing the nuances of teaching that are not part of teacher-education programs and crash courses that lead to teacher certification. Reality pedagogy considers the range of emotions that new teachers experience when embarking on their careers but also acknowledges the experiences that veteran teachers may have had that left them jaded. Most importantly, it begins with the acceptance of the often overlooked fact that there are cultural differences between students and their teachers that make it difficult for teachers to be reflective and effective, while providing a set of steps that allow these misalignments to be overcome.

Reality pedagogy does not draw its cues for teaching from "classroom experts" who are far removed from real schools, or from researchers who make suggestions for the best ways to teach "urban," "suburban," and "rural" youth based on their perceptions of what makes sense for classrooms. Rather, it focuses on teaching and learning as it is successfully practiced within communities physically outside of, and oftentimes beyond, the school. Rather than give teachers a set of tools to implement and hope that these approaches meet the specific needs of urban youth and their teachers in particular classrooms, reality pedagogy provides educators with a mechanism for developing approaches to teaching that meet the specific needs of the students sitting in front of them. [W]e will [later]delve into this approach and outline how it serves as a way for white folks who teach in the hood—and the rest of y'all too—to improve their pedagogy.

Endnotes

1. Adrienne Rich, *Blood, Bread, and Poetry: Selected Prose, 1979–1985* (New York: Norton, 1986).
2. Kelly Oliver, *The Colonization of Psychic Space: A Psychoanalytic Social Theory of Oppression* (Minneapolis: University of Minnesota Press, 2004).
3. Ralph Ellison, *Invisible Man* (New York: Random House, 1952), 1.
4. John R. Searle, *The Construction of Social Reality* (New York: Free Press, 1995), 15.
5. See Eduardo Duran, *Healing the Soul Wound: Counseling with American Indians and Other Native Peoples* (New York: Teachers College Press, 2006); Mark Findlay, *The Globalisation of Crime: Understanding Transitional Relationships in Context* (Cambridge, UK: Cambridge University Press, 1999).

Reading 1B

Courage
Teach without Fear

Christopher Emdin

On my first day as a teacher, after the principal led me and three other beginning teachers on a final tour of the school, I joined the rest of the faculty in the auditorium, preparing for the students to arrive. As we waited for the doors to open, the other new teachers and I struggled to mask the emotions that roiled beneath our calm facades. At one point, we peered between the bars on the windows of the auditorium to catch a glimpse of the students who were lined up against a graffiti-stained wall outside the school building. There they stood, in their first-day-of-school outfits: brand-new gleaming sneakers in an array of bright colors and perfectly coordinated clothes, experiencing a bevy of emotions themselves, poised to meet their new teachers.

A few feet from the auditorium, metal detectors adorned the big metal doors that the students would soon walk through. As the queue outside the door grew, so did the sound of the students' voices, and with them, the tension inside the room as the huge clock on the auditorium wall slowly ticked to 8:30. A fellow new teacher, impeccably dressed in the principal's recommended khakis and blazer, looked up at me. "Do you hear them out there?" she asked nervously as the school doors opened and the students began to stream in.

I responded to her question with a half-smile and shrug, intended to show that I wasn't intimidated. On the inside, it was a different story. I had heard about how tough these "urban kids" were going to be. At one point, I realized that my nervousness was evident as I observed my hand tremble; I quickly slipped it into my pocket. The fact that I had lived in neighborhoods just like the one in which the school stood, and may have walked past these students

Christopher Emdin, "Courage: Teach without Fear," *For White Folks Who Teach in the Hood...and the Rest of Y'all Too*, pp. 31-43, 212. Copyright © 2016 by Beacon Press. Reprinted with permission.

hundreds of times as I strode up and down these same streets, did nothing to calm my nerves. Somehow, the stories about angry and violent urban youth who did not want to be in school and did not want to learn stripped them of their humanity, erasing the reality that they were just children on the first day of school.

Fear-Based Narratives

The stereotypes we brought with us into that school auditorium shaped our understandings not only of the students we would be teaching but also of what it means to teach. Rather than approach teaching with the confidence that comes from knowing your mission and the joy of being placed in a school where one can fulfill it, we approached the arrival of the students with an unhealthy apprehension about what the next academic year would bring. We hyper-analyzed everything the students brought to the school in search of anything that would affirm the negative stories we had heard about them. Before they even spoke, we read their exchanges with each other and marked them as either teachable or not. We gave each other knowing glances based on how students walked through the auditorium. We would breathe a collective sigh of relief when a student appeared to be "teachable," and nod knowingly when a student looked like trouble. The seemingly shy and demure students, by virtue of not being the prototypical urban student described to us by the media and in popular narratives, became the teachable ones. These students elicited smiles and positive emotions. On the other hand, the students who spoke too loudly and seemed to be exuding too much confidence or "urbanness" were immediately judged "problem students."

The process of identifying the good and bad students became a game of sorts for me and the other new teachers. What we didn't realize as we began to play this game was that our seemingly impromptu categorizations of young people came from very real ideas about youth that we had subconsciously ingested. As we got deeper into this game, its complexity slowly revealed itself. The more my peers and I became preoccupied with positioning students as teachable or not, the more invested we became in the process. Our everyday conversations in our first year of teaching became reaffirmations of the categorizations we had developed on the first day. We were in many ways no different than European settlers in their first interactions with the indigenous, sharing observations of their unrefined culture and violent nature. We spent our lunch meetings and after-school professional-development sessions trying to one-up each other with stories about how challenging our students were. We spent so much time and energy exaggerating these stories that we became distracted from our initial goal to affect change. Our preoccupation with positioning ourselves as good guys in a war against the young people meant that we were fulfilling our chief function as cogs in the urban-education machine. The more we told tales of dysfunction, the more we worked to maintain it.

This process eroded the unbridled passion that brought us into the field of education, transforming us into agents of a traditional school culture that worked against young people.

The process was subtle and took different forms for each of the teachers who stood in the auditorium that morning. For many of the white teachers, the process held an unmistakable element of racism. Phrases like "these kids" or "those kids" were often clearly code words for bad black and brown children.

The teachers' venting sessions reminded me of my experiences in high school and how I was forced to obey rules without an opportunity to question whether they supported the way I learned. As a high school student, the more I engaged in school, the more I learned about the rules that guided the institution and realized that they ran counter to the ways I experienced the world. The more I realized that there was a gap between who I was as a young black man and who the institution and the teachers wanted me to be, the more I rebelled against school and all it represented. In many ways, this is where the association between being academically successful and "acting white," studied by education researchers like John Ogbu, comes from.[1] These scholars argue that black youth view doing well in school as acting white, without considering that teachers may perceive being black as not wanting to do well in school. The issue is not that youth of color see academic success as limited to whites. It is that they typically see white teachers as enforcers of rules that are unrelated to the actual teaching and learning process. Consequently, they respond negatively to whatever structures these teachers value even at the expense of their own academic success.

In my experiences in school, I underperformed in classes in which teachers privileged ways of engaging with content that stifled my creativity and did well in classes where I wasn't forced to obey rules, but had an opportunity to learn. By my final year of high school, I had been identified as a troublemaker even though I wanted to go to college. Once I left high school, and with the constant reminder and awareness that I needed an education in order to be successful in the future, I learned to assimilate into the culture of traditional schooling. Unfortunately, this process meant that I spent almost all of my time in my final year of high school working to erase my everyday realities and dismiss the knowledge that I gained in my out-of-school world. The process of indoctrination was difficult, and I often rebelled against it. On occasion, when the work of conforming got too taxing, I would ask teachers questions to challenge the structures they had in place in the hope of improving the classroom environment. However, questions like, "Can we stand up and stretch if we need to?" were met with firm requests to sit back down and looks from the teacher that said much more about what the teachers thought of me than any words could. In response, I would take the bathroom pass and walk the hallways, thinking that I had won a game of sorts with the teacher. I got a chance to walk around and stretch and there was nothing that could be done about it.

Unbeknownst to me, I was the loser in a larger game, missing out on what was being taught in the classroom and drawn into another game of cat and mouse with security officials who patrolled the building in search of students like me who were leaving class out of boredom, frustration, or just a chance to breathe. Either way, all of us who left our classrooms in silent protest against the oppressive structure of the classroom came to a point where we considered whether or not it was easier to sit in class and play the game of attentive student or challenge the rules that were being enforced by the teachers. A few decided to play the game, but many more either did not, or could not. The ones who played graduated high school, went on to college, and some even became teachers.

Years later, when I became a teacher, I learned much about the structure of urban schools and grew to become the embodiment of the very teachers who placed me in the vice that had squeezed all of the fight out of me as a student. Then, as I'd navigated the landscape of formal education and played a game whose rules were enforced largely by white folks who teach in the hood, I became conditioned to be a "proper student" and began to lose value for pieces of myself that previously defined me. My unabashed urbanness—loud, conspicuous, and questioning of authority—became lost. This was encouraged when I got into the teaching profession. When I took my first job in a school with students whose faces looked much like mine, the most memorable advice I received from an older teacher was, "You look too much like them, and they won't take you seriously. Hold your ground, and don't smile till November." To be an effective black male educator for youth of color, I was being advised to erase pieces of myself and render significant pieces of who I was invisible. That's what was needed to enter into teaching, which was increasingly being presented as a war against young people.

For my closest teacher colleague who stood in the auditorium with me when we began our careers, recruitment into the army against urban youth began when, as a young person, she was taught to "be a good person" and "leave a mark on the world." She was white and from a middle-class background and had seen pictures of her parents when they were in their twenties feeding poor children in Africa on missionary trips. She was chosen to teach in the school based on her good grades and "change the world" attitude as identified by a teacher-recruitment program that brought white folks to teach in the hood. A recent college graduate from a private liberal arts university, she was inspired by the idea of giving back to poor communities. She took the job to get the free master's degree that many new urban teachers receive, but was drawn into the profession by the opportunity to experience some version of her parents' missionary trips. The exotic images from her parents' photographs could be played out in her life through urban America, and her privilege had created a guilt that could be eased by teaching the poor black and brown kids in her classroom.

In our conversations, we explored our experiences on the path to becoming urban educators, discussed our motivations for teaching, our experiences thus far, and finally, the advice we had received to prepare us to successfully do the work we both believed we were called to do. I had been trained my entire life to believe that being something other than who I truly was would make me a better person. She had been trained to be herself and help the "less fortunate." Though our motivations and experiences were different, in the course of our conversations we learned that we had one thing in common: the constant reminder by peers, family members, teachers, and now school administrators to see urban youth of color as a group that is potentially dangerous and needs to be saved from themselves. We were both told not to express too much emotion with students or be too friendly with them. I was told to "stand your ground when they test you," "don't let them know anything about your life so they don't get too familiar," and "remember that there is nothing wrong with being mean." Everyone from whom we solicited advice shared a variation of the phrase "Don't smile till November."

The phrase was simple and memorable, and easily took hold in the hearts and minds of both my new colleague and myself. It became our mantra. In tense and uncomfortable moments, when students raised their voices and threats were hurled our way, it gave us boldness and confidence. We would share the same knowing glances that helped us to categorize students as teachable or not on the first day to reaffirm our stances as no-nonsense educators. The phrase kept us standing when our knees wobbled in the school auditorium on our first day of teaching and made us confident past November. Unfortunately, this same mantra required us to remove all emotion from our teaching. It turned us from passionate educators into automatons who worked to maintain the school's structures and inequities. Rather than face our fears, the mantra helped us to mask them. And because being in touch with one's emotions is the key to moving from the classroom (place) to the spaces where the students are, our students were invisible to us.

Facing Fear: Before and Beyond November

To be an educator in America today means that your students' test scores, GPAs, and graduation rates are the primary measures of your effectiveness. Standardized exams drive everything from curriculum to teaching. As a result, many teachers believe that anything aside from teaching to the test will be detrimental to students and teachers alike. This makes it easy for some educators to ascribe to the "Don't smile till November" mantra. Teachers become adept at creating high-pressure classrooms focused more on testing than teaching. Teachers are reduced to test-prep machines.

White folks who teach in the hood are particularly prone to this sort of rote model. This is especially the case if they are convinced that having all students pass tests creates some form of equity. In these cases they are so married to a curriculum that is sold as the only path to passing the test that there is no willingness to deviate from it even if it is harming students. Furthermore, teaching to an exam and strictly following a curriculum makes it easier for these teachers to remain emotionally disconnected from students.

Consider a scenario where a group of teachers I was working with were expected to teach a unit on Europe during the semester. As I worked with the teachers to plan for the unit, one of them began telling the group about a European tour she took with her family when she was a teenager. As the teachers individually planned their lessons, she spoke enthusiastically about the trip and shared a lot of powerful and engaging stories that merged with the themes in the unit. As the planning session ended, the teachers thanked her for her stories and headed to their respective classes with the lessons they had worked on in tow.

Over the course of the next week, I visited a number of these teachers' classes and found all of their lessons to be similar. This was even the case when I went to the class of the teacher who had entertained us with her travel stories. None of her amazing stories had made it into her lesson. When I asked her why this was the case, she threw out a number of excuses that included not wanting to get too personal with her students, not wanting to be perceived as bragging, only having enough time in the lesson to cover what she was expected to, and wanting to follow the unit she was given by the school administration. Despite my efforts to convince the teacher that her personal stories could have helped her engage her students, she was adamant in her belief that sharing them would have undermined her in some way. This same teacher was one of many who later complained at the end of the academic year about how poorly students did on the standardized test she was so intent on teaching to.

In a related scenario, after working with a science teacher who complained incessantly that she needed glassware like beakers and pipettes in order to engage her students in science, I convinced the school administration to purchase these materials for her classes. Because funding for such an acquisition was a challenge, I actually bought some of the requested materials on my own. Eventually, after a few months, a number of lab materials were delivered to the teacher's classroom. I excitedly visited her classroom week after week to see what impact the new materials were having on science instruction, but a month went by and the materials still had not been put to use. Frustrated, I finally asked her what was up. After a long pause, she responded by saying that she'd had a change of heart and wasn't sure that the students were ready to use the items. She worried they might be used as weapons. What if the students broke the glass and used it to cut each other? Obviously, in constructing this narrative she was guided by her perception of her students as potentially violent. Unfortunately, their teacher's presuppositions had robbed these students of a promising learning opportunity.

In each of the scenarios described above, the white teachers held perceptions about the students and the type of instruction they needed that were rooted in bias. The notion that students wouldn't respond to powerful personal stories or would resort to violence if given the opportunity is clearly rooted in stereotypes about poverty, and in these cases black and brown youth of color. These biases were then used to justify ineffective teaching that is absolved from critique because of its supposed alignment to standardized exams. In reality, the persistence of achievement gaps proves that teaching that is not personalized and not hands-on (as is most teaching in traditional urban schools) does not equate to success on standardized exams. It also should lead to conversations about how these approaches to teaching actually support the persistence of the gaps they are designed to close.

When teaching doesn't connect to students, it is perceived as not belonging to them. Students begin to use phrases like "your exam" or "their test" when describing the assessments they are required to take, signaling to the educators that there is no vested interest in the test or their success on it. These same students exhibit resilience, dedication, and hard work in a number of tasks in their neighborhoods and devote hours on end to supporting each other in activities that have real meaning.

I remember one eighth-grade student I taught who had perfect attendance at school but whom I had identified as disconnected and disinterested in my class. I ran into her a few years later at a movie theater housed in a local shopping mall. When I recognized her from a few feet away, she tried to avoid eye contact with me and turned toward the concession stand. It was pretty obvious that she wasn't interested in reminiscing about old times. Taking the hint, I turned in the opposite direction and slowly attempted to make my way out of the theater. As I did so, one of the small children she had with her broke free and came running in my direction. My former student lunged after him and we ended up almost running into each other. I smiled and said hello, she did the same, and I bent over to introduce myself to the boy who was now clutching her leg while narrowly missing the swinging leg of the child she held in her arms. Her other hand clutching another child's hand, she introduced me to her son, little brother, and sister. I quickly calculated that she was now a junior in high school and asked her how school was going. She told me that she was the primary caregiver to her two younger siblings, since her mother had passed away during the year I was her teacher. She spoke to me about the declining health of her grandmother, whom she lived with, and of her decision to stay in school because she wanted to make something of her life. About her current high school experience, she then said, "All those white teachers be acting just like you, just meaner." In that moment, she uncovered how prevalent that "mean" style of teaching was, but also displayed her incredible resilience. I had perceived her as disconnected and disinterested in school, even though she was obviously the opposite of that. Unfortunately, I'd had no structures in place at the time to forge a connection with this student and allow her to tap into the resilience that brought her to school every day and help her apply it in my class.

I understand the pressures teachers are under and the challenges they face meeting high standards for success on measures that seem insurmountable. The current landscape of urban education, which holds teachers accountable for student outcomes while failing to equip teachers with the tools to meet these outcomes is paralyzing. However, the key to getting students to be academically successful (even if the teacher decides that success means passing an exam), is not to teach directly to the assessment or to the curriculum, but to teach *directly to the students*. Every educator who works with the neoindigenous must first recognize their students' neoindigeneity and teach from the standpoint of an ally who is working with them to reclaim their humanity.

To be an ally to the neoindigenous, the teacher must unpack the indoctrination that we have all been subject to. For white folks who teach in the hood, this may require a much more intense unpacking. For me, this meant taking the time to analyze why I was initially scared of my students and moving beyond that fear, acknowledging that getting to know my students and having them know me may alter the power structure and affect classroom management.

For many teachers, the school day has devolved into nothing more than a series of routines. If students are seated and quiet during most of the lesson, and teachers only have to yell enough times to get a sore throat once or twice a month, they view themselves as successful. They may not be reaching the students, or inspiring them to value education, but they rest comfortably knowing that they are doing their job as defined by the school. The lessons are scripted and the students are quiet. One group of students trickles in begrudgingly at the sound of the bell, and the same group pushes out of the class hastily at the sound of another bell. A dissenter among the group occasionally steps out of line and a referral is written or security is called. The pattern continues across classrooms throughout the day, and as long as there isn't an emergency, everything is perceived to be okay. This routine is familiar to many urban educators and allows them to maintain that things are not as bad as they could be rather than focus on how they should be. In this way, we become comfortable with dysfunctional teaching.

In my view, we do not see daily emergencies because we are conditioned to the norms of teaching and learning that are in themselves in a state of emergency. The entire system of urban education is failing youth of color by any number of criteria, the structure of the traditional urban school privileges poor teaching practices, these practices trigger responses from students that reflect "poor behavior," the poor behavior triggers deeply entrenched biases that teachers hold, and when this triggering of biases is coupled with the cycling in and out of white folks to teach in the hood, former teachers with activated biases leave urban classrooms to become policymakers and education experts who do not believe in young people or their communities. In response, I suggest an approach to urban education that benefits the two most significant parties in the traditional school—the student and the teacher—an approach to teaching and learning that not only considers what is right for students, but what makes the teacher most effective and fulfilled. This vision of teaching doesn't hide the fact that challenges in urban education persist because of our collective investment in maintaining a system that is intent on forcing brilliance to silence itself and then dealing with the varied repercussions. Once educators recognize that they are biased against forms of brilliance other than their own, they can finally begin to truly teach.

The new teachers I stood with in that auditorium on the first day of school, the teacher who failed to share with her students her stories about traveling in Europe, and the one who let fear stand in the way of providing her students with lab materials that would engage them in science—all of us had something in common. Our understandings of who was and wasn't a good student were rooted less in our experiences with urban students and more on our perceptions of them, which were largely based on a flawed narrative.

In my experience, having attended an urban public school and having taught in one years later, I found that not challenging the prevailing narrative about urban students led me to teach in ways that would not have worked for me when I was a student. If the teenage me had walked into the auditorium in which I stood on my first day as a teacher, the adult me would have judged my teenage self as unprepared for learning and not properly equipped for being intellectually challenged; from the way I looked and acted, I would have been labeled "trouble." On the path to becoming a teacher, I had learned to shed all elements of my teenage self. Not being able to smile till November robbed me of the opportunity of seeing myself in the students in front of me. Instead, the structures of schooling forced me to devalue anyone who brought any semblance of my teenage self into the present-day classroom. Today, with thousands of hours of teacher observations under my belt and having spent innumerable hours reflecting back on my own teaching, it is clear to me how teachers develop and maintain a deficit view of students. This is particularly evident when I think of how teachers of color have been taught to manage the behavior of students who do look like them, despite knowing that their neoindigeneity requires their voices being heard and their ideas validated.

The work for teachers becomes developing the self-reflection necessary to deconstruct the ways that media messages, other teachers' negative (often exaggerated) stories, and their own need to be the hero affects how they see and teach students. The teacher must work to ensure that the institution does not absolve them of the responsibility to acknowledge the baggage they bring to the classroom and analyze how that might affect student achievement. Without teachers recognizing the biases they hold and how these biases impact the ways they see and teach students, there is no starting point to changing the dismal statistics related to the academic underperformance of urban youth.

Endnote

1. See, inter alia, John Ogbu, *Black American Students in an Affluent Suburb: A Study of Academic Disengagement* (Mahwah, NJ: Erlbaum, 2003).

Reading 2

Teaching

Chris Mercagliano

Man is born like a garden ready planted and sown.
—William Blake

EVERY SO OFTEN, MISSY, WHO DIRECTS the preschool now, gets out her easel and her sketchbook and sets up shop in a quiet corner of one of the downstairs classrooms. She closes the door, rigs up a good, bright light next to the subject's stool, sharpens up her set of artist pencils and voilà: an instant portrait studio.

Before long kids are clamoring to have Missy draw them; sometimes it takes a solid week or more for her to get everyone in. Usually I or another downstairs teacher will take her place upstairs so that she can stay in her studio and gradually work her way through the line of eager young models.

What Missy doesn't tell the kids is that this is her art class. She is showing them how to draw.

The teaching process begins with Missy's own feeling for her craft. She loves doing portraits and her joy quickly expands to fill the room. For her subjects, the experience of being drawn, of watching their own image slowly appear on Missy's easel, is enthralling. It's like seeing a photograph magically materialize in a darkroom developing pan.

Missy is careful to position herself so that the kids have a clear view of her as she draws. Probably without even realizing, they are watching her motions and mannerisms intently. A little like a chatty hairdresser, Missy keeps up a light banter to quell impatience and prevent the atmosphere from getting too serious. She points out to each subject the items of distinction in their features

Chris Mercagliano, "Teaching," *Making It Up as We Go Along: The Story of Albany Free School*, pp. 115-122. Copyright © 1998 by Chris Mercagliano.

as she draws them, describes her movements with the pencil, and alternately remains quiet as she sketches away with great concentration.

Just like artists in Central Park, Missy attracts a crowd while she works. Her enjoyment is contagious. She doesn't mind the gang of kids gathered around to watch, because she knows that just like her subject, the onlookers are intently studying her technique.

On the second or third day of the run, you'll find Missy seated on the subject's stool. Her former subject is now her student and she might, if the mood is right, begin to give some light instruction. How much directed teaching she will do will depend on the needs and wishes of each individual child, and on the chemistry between student and teacher.

Before it's all over, the room will be full of kids drawing other kids, or drawing themselves, and Missy will be floating around answering questions and giving encouragement. The portrait light—now lights—will stay on continuously. A display wall will quickly fill with art work of extraordinary quality. And the drawings won't be coming from a hand-picked group of precocious young artists but from whoever decided to hang around and try it out for themselves. Always most impressive to me are the sketches done by kids who don't necessarily have a gift for portraiture. Their leap in skill during that single week with Missy is nothing short of remarkable.

The class ends when there aren't any more portraits to be drawn. There's no art show and no prizes. Missy simply thanks everybody for a great time, packs up her things, and goes back upstairs to her little ones.

MANY MIGHT THINK a loose and open-ended approach to teaching is fine in areas like art, but what about hard-core skills areas like reading, writing, and arithmetic? Or science or history? Don't they require more rigor and regimen?

The answer, I think, is an unqualified maybe. Or a hearty it all depends. But certainly not necessarily, as the nation's curriculum experts would have us all believe. For instance, when Nancy is teaching reading, oftentimes she just reads aloud to her students. She selects good, compelling stuff, or the kids bring in favorite selections of their own. And just as Missy draws, Nancy reads with excitement and passion. Kids gather round close to her and she changes expressions and voices to bring the characters to life right there in the room. There's no time limit either; she usually doesn't stop until everyone's too tired to listen any more.

Sometimes Nancy mixes in instruction. She teaches phonics, gets students to read along with her, writes down their stories and has them read them back, encourages them to create their own newspapers and magazines. It was Nancy who helped the kids make [a] hand-powered "television" [...], which told each episode in subtitles. Without a whole lot of fanfare she posts their stories and poems on the walls, and helps each of them to maintain an active file of their work on the classroom Macintosh. And Nancy never forgets that play is a huge component of the learning process. She doesn't want the kids to think of reading as hard work.

Meanwhile, dozens of young children learn to read under her auspices without necessarily having been "taught." Some kids need a lot of help learning to read, others little or none at all. Woody, who has been teaching reading for more than fifty years at the Peninsula School, one of the nation's longest-running alternative schools, states emphatically that there are as many ways to teach reading as there are students to learn. It is imperative, she says, for a teacher to respect the individuality of every student, to help them find, in her words, "the magic way" that works for them.

Mary preferred a mythological approach to teaching. One year, for example, she and a group of kids invented a magical adventure game against which the more recent "Dungeons and Dragons" would pale by comparison. Dubbed "The Cellar Adventure," the game was very Tolkienesque and involved hunting buried treasure in a mysterious land filled with ogres and dragons. First, they wrote out the game's rules, characters, and story line, and even created maps. Then they spent a great many days enacting the drama in real life. Suddenly the school's dark, dirt-floored cellar—accessible only by a heavy trap door—became its most popular and exciting classroom.

The game involved reading and writing, but that's not really why Mary cooked it up. She was operating according to her keen awareness that awakened and engaged children learn better. She also understood the almost limitless power inherent in a group process where, when it is a mutually supportive one, everyone brings out the best in each other. So her first order of business every year was to help kids form real working teams; then as time passed, to stop whenever necessary to repair any tears in the fabric that might have occurred along the way. No one ever got left behind, and whenever someone would begin to drift away, she would turn it over to the rest of the group to bring the odd child out back into the circle. The kids responded magnificently to the challenge of this level of responsibility, in part, I surmise, because it galvanized in them a feeling that it was *their* class, and not just Mary's.

What always amazed me the most about Mary's teaching style was her indomitable belief in every student's ability to succeed. She absolutely refused to give up on anyone. Once, before she started the Free School, while still teaching at a small private school in then-segregated Texas in the early 1960s, she took under her wing a black high school student who was struggling academically. Even though the young man wasn't keeping up in his standard subjects, he elected to join Mary's Latin class. He then proceeded not only to become accomplished in that classical language, but to transfer the model of competence he had internalized there to other areas—to such an extent that he was able to go on to college and then to a successful professional career. Now, he writes to Mary each Christmas to fill her in on the latest news of his life and to thank her for the difference she made in it. Mary would be the first to say that her former student deserves all the credit for his amazing turnaround, and of course that is so. Nevertheless, the power of the role of teacher, properly played, must never be overlooked.

JOHN GATTO WRITES in *The Empty Child*: "Kids don't resist learning; they resist teaching." A few years earlier, Herb Kohl wrote an entire book with the very same thesis. Called *I Won't Learn From You*, it explores the tremendous damage done to children in our schools by negative teaching. Just as the title suggests, Kohl says that the poor performance of a great many students is often not due to any shortcoming on their part. Rather it is an expression of their will to resist the control of adults who they feel do not have their best interests at heart.

The infamous Pygmalion in the Classroom study, where, unbeknownst to their teachers, the test scores of two incoming fourth-grade groups—one high-achieving, the other low—were reversed, provides a sobering empirical demonstration of the power a teacher's attitude toward his or her students can have over them. After a fairly brief interval with their new teachers, the children were tested again, and lo and behold, the former high achievers were suddenly performing at the level of the former low achievers and vice versa.

It is perhaps this very situation in the nation's schools, where our children are daily held hostage to the beliefs and expectations of a single adult—who increasingly remains a remote stranger in their lives—that has led people like Mary to start their own schools, or hundreds of thousands of homeschooling families to abandon the idea of school altogether. Whether at home, or in the wide array of alternative schools that now dot the nation, a vastly different model of teaching—including self-teaching—is at work.

It derives from a very different model of learning, one based on a fundamental respect for the centrality of the learner in the teaching/learning process. Such a shift of emphasis from teacher to learner in no way diminishes the value of good teaching and good teachers. There will always be a place in this world for people who can effectively teach others, whether those teachers wear some kind of professional badge or not. Frank, who calls himself a craftsman, not a teacher, was able to teach Jesse a set of valuable manual skills; at the same time, he helped Jesse do some important growing up.

The majority of practitioners in all of the varied alternatives to conventional schooling—homeschoolers very much included—operates according to a model of learning that, above all, honors the personhood of the learner. It reviles against coercion and respects the right of the learner to codetermine the conditions under which he or she will engage in the process. It holds volition and choice paramount. It maintains a bedrock faith in every child's inborn desire to learn and grow, to become knowledgeable, effective, and competent. And finally, it recognizes the validity of independent learning and self-teaching, where teacher and learner simply occupy the same being.

Recent brain/mind research is on the verge of confirming approaches to education that replace coercion with free choice, teacher-centeredness with child-centeredness, competition with cooperation, enforced togetherness with opportunities for solitary pursuits, management with autonomy, memorization with exploration and discovery, grading with self-assessment, and obligation with exuberance.

Joseph Chilton Pearce writes extensively about the emerging new biology and field theory-based model of learning and human intelligence in *Evolution's End*, a title he chose to convey his growing concern over humanity's failure, thus far, to utilize the immense potential of the mind. Pearce states that all human knowledge is, in fact, innate, and that what we call learning is actually a process whereby deeply embedded development unfolds from the inside out in response to the right cues from the environment.

Echoing Howard Gardiner, Pearce views each individual as a collection of potential intelligences, and translating them from mere potentiality into our personal experience of them is what some call child development, or others education. Further, writes Pearce: "Nature's agenda unfolds these intelligences for their development within us at a time appropriate to each." We can fail to nurture an intelligence by pushing it too soon, waiting too long, or ignoring it altogether. All the infant/child wants to do is what nature intended, which is to build up structures of knowledge; all that he or she needs to do that is a sufficiently stimulating environment, or in Pearce's words, "to be surrounded by mature, intelligent intellects, open to mind's possibilities and tempered by heart's wisdom, recognizing that to the human all may be possible."

If we look to the ongoing research into the abundant intelligence with which babies are born, this whole idea of innate knowing begins to sound a lot less mystical. For instance, we now know that a healthy newborn baby (who has not been excessively traumatized during the birth process) will respond immediately to the image of a human face if held at a distance of six to twelve inches—the distance between a mother's face and nursing breast—since this genetically encoded visual circuit has already been hardwired for just that purpose.

Next, the stimulus of the initial face recognition will trigger the ripening of the baby's entire visual apparatus, which will then become the key that begins unlocking myriad doors in the infant's rapidly expanding intellect. The very same is true for the development of language, whose building blocks are equally hardwired into a baby's neural circuitry and are only waiting for the appropriate environmental stimuli in order to begin gradually coalescing and unfolding into articulate speech.

Does this notion of "hardwired" intelligence negate the importance of teaching? Hardly, because it is nature's imperative, according to Pearce, that no human learning occur without a stimulus from an already mature form of that particular intelligence. The kind of stimulus he is referring to, however, is anything but mechanical or one-dimensional; rather it is holographic. Teachers influence students on a myriad of subtle—or not so subtle—levels, as the "Pygmalian" study so dramatically confirms. Here Pearce reminds us how it is estimated that 95 percent of all learning takes place below the level of conscious awareness, meaning that students in a teacher/student interaction are taking in far more than just information or the demonstration of a particular skill. They are also affected by teachers' moods, beliefs, and attitudes, as well as by how teachers feel about themselves, their students, and what they are teaching.

As Pearce says, "Teachers teach who they are"—meaning that beneath all of the trappings, teachers teach by modeling, not by instructing, managing, or evaluating student performance, the foundations of the role as it is typically practiced in conventional school settings. Therefore, teaching can no longer be viewed simply as a process whereby one person more skilled than another breaks down a subject or a procedure into small enough pieces for the student to digest successfully.

We urgently need a new vocabulary to describe the teaching/learning interface. The old Western scientific, cause-and-effect paradigm doesn't suffice anymore, since we have expanded our understanding of the teaching/learning process to the point where we know it isn't something that one person does to another, but rather is a form of interactive collaboration occurring on many different levels. Since the knowledge and skills we previously believed needed to be taught to the student are already there waiting to be awakened, we can no longer accept the old schooling premise that the teacher is the cause and the student is the effect of the learning process.

Thus, when Missy, Nancy, and Mary are teaching children in the Free School, they are conscious of the importance of being present with the fullness of themselves. Missy realizes she isn't just teaching the *doing*—the skills and techniques—of drawing, rather she is modeling *being* an artist and loving art. She knows she is also modeling herself, and so at any given moment there might occur levels of sharing between her and the students that outwardly might have little to do with the "subject" of art.

The same is true for Nancy when she is teaching reading. What she is really doing is modeling the beauty, power, joy, and ease of reading. She's showing the kids for whom reading might not come as easily that reading is a pleasure, not a struggle. She never tries to force anyone to go any faster than they are currently ready, willing, or able to go. And like Missy, she's always available with her full self.

Whenever Mary teaches, and she still does from time to time, what she is actually doing is leading kids on a personal quest to discover how to embrace the totality of themselves, no-holds-barred. That is the way she has always lived her own life and kids instinctively understand and respond to her example.

THE PROPOSITION THAT a true teacher is a fully holistic model and not merely a taskmaster or a classroom manager means it is impossible for teachers to lead their students any farther than they have already taken themselves. One simply cannot model something one hasn't already experienced oneself. This, then, leads to the imperative that all of us who consider ourselves teachers, especially good ones, not only make sure we are fluent with the material we are teaching, but that we also pay careful attention to our own emotional health, as well as other matters of personal growth and development—and that we continue to do this on an ongoing basis. Everyone working with children of any age must strive to be whole persons. And this doesn't just include teachers in schools. Parents are—and should always be—among their kids' most important teachers.

For this reason more than any other Mary suggested in the school's early days that we institute a weekly personal growth group. "Group," as we simply call it, began in 1974, and has met nearly every Wednesday evening ever since. Here is where we work on our own personal life-issues and problems as they arise, as well as where we are able to delve more deeply into the emotional and spiritual dimensions of our evolving selves.

It is also here that we resolve the interpersonal conflicts that inevitably result from working together so closely. The work we do individually and together in group is instrumental in helping us keep our minds and hearts open to the kids we are coming into such close contact with every day in school.

I have a friend named John Lawry, who teaches future teachers at Marymount College in Poughkeepsie, New York. He once wrote an article, which he has since expanded into book-length form, entitled *"Caritas* in the Classroom: The Opening of the American Student's Heart." In it he confirms my belief—one that Joseph Chilton Pearce would readily embrace—in the primacy of openheartedness in the teaching process.

Professor Lawry writes that it is peculiar to the West to bypass the emotional connection between student and teacher. The article sprang from a personal discovery that his own classroom was transformed as he began reversing this tradition. He found that when he stepped from behind his mask of professional composure and began revealing his own emotional life, and when he started asking his students how they were feeling about themselves and their lives, their engagement in the learning process increased dramatically. Here he was modeling for them how to engage their students in the many years to come.

Lawry also refers to a little-known study showing that students of teachers who measure high in qualities such as empathy, psychological integrity, and positive regard have significantly better standardized test scores than students of teachers who measure low in those areas. While test scores can be interpreted in myriad ways for as many reasons, shouldn't it be obvious that openhearted teachers engender openhearted students, who in turn become more effective learners?

I think so.

Reading 3

Building a Caring Classroom That Supports Achievement

Carl A. Grant and Christine E. Sleeter

This [reading] will help you answer the following questions:
- How do fantastic teachers develop positive student–teacher rapport?
- What does it mean to be a caring teacher?
- How can I use conflict resolution and for what purposes?
- How can I use cooperative learning effectively?
- How can I conduct class meetings effectively?
- How can I help students address prejudice and stereotyping?

[... You] examined yourself, students, and student-centered teaching as the basis for achievement, and you looked at classrooms in their wider social and historical context. Now, it is time to move into the classroom, roll up our sleeves, and begin to build practice. Where do we start?

We believe the best place to start is with relationships, because they form the foundation for everything else that happens in the classroom. For students, learning involves taking risks—trying out new ideas, skills, and even identities, trusting that the teacher truly has their best interests at heart and that classroom peers will support rather than discourage risk taking. As Meier (2002) noted,

> Learning happens fastest when the novices trust the setting so much that they aren't afraid to take risks, make mistakes, or do something dumb. Learning works best, in fact, when the very idea that it's risky hasn't even occurred to kids.
>
> (p. 18)

Teachers are responsible for building relationships that sustain learning and growth and the risk taking involved. But for teachers, building relationships involves risks, too, because caring exposes us emotionally.

Building trust, authentic caring, and trusting relationships involve work. Most educators agree that care is essential to good teaching. Care not only supports learning and achievement but is also the fundamental glue that holds societies together. Therefore, to help you get started, the first section of the [reading] will unpack what it means to "care," applying this concept to teacher–student and student–student relationships. Then, the [reading] will develop three building blocks:

Building Block 6: Using Conflict Resolution
Building Block 7: Addressing Prejudice and Stereotyping
Building Block 8: Using Cooperative Learning

Most of the reflections in this [reading] involve you in analyzing ideas or connecting them with your own experiences. But for a few of them, you will need access to the following:

- The Internet (for Reflections 3.7 and 3.12);
- Three people of any age to interview (for Reflection 3.3); and
- About five young people you can talk with (for Reflection 3.8).

Care and Relationships in School

A study in the 1990s asked everyone (students, teachers, custodians, cafeteria workers, etc.) inside four schools in Southern California: "What is the central problem of schooling?" Interpersonal relationships—caring—emerged as the primary concern. People said that their best experiences in schools involved other people who cared, listened, and respected them. But they also noted that there was too little time throughout the day to cultivate personal relationships and that too much fear and misunderstanding got in the way. Race, culture, and class were the second main concerns because these determined who had access to the most satisfying academic experiences and who felt understood and supported in school. One student summed up the research by saying, "This place hurts my spirit" (Institute for Education in Transformation, 1992).

Student Dialogue 3.1

Celia: Oh, that reminds me so much of my junior high! It was a mixed school, but there was a real pecking order. Someone like me with brown skin and a Spanish accent was seen as lower than low. I hated school then.

Gilbert: I wouldn't say I hated school or that it hurt my spirit. I've got a pretty tough spirit. But I know quite a few kids who never made it to tenth grade because they couldn't be themselves in school. They had to choose between being themselves or being a student. The way the school defined "student," they couldn't be both.

Lisa: I want to ask you two about your experiences because mine might have been different. But first I want to say that I'm glad we are dealing with trust building before getting into more heavy-duty topics. [Earlier] was rough, and I don't know you two very well. Until I know you won't laugh at me, or think I'm racist or stuck up or something, I watch what I say.

Celia: I feel the same way. I don't worry about being seen as racist, but I worry about sounding dumb. I need to know someone and trust that person before I open up very much.

Lisa and Celia echo the feelings of many students. They want to speak up during class discussions but are concerned about what others will think about their comments and actions. Building trust and providing a safe space, therefore, are the first order of business to the establishment of a productive learning environment. In addition, "race" arguably is the most difficult topic for a mixed racial and ethnic group of Americans to discuss. Gilbert's point about "being oneself" is also a challenge because of peer pressure and pressure from the school and teachers to conform to the school's way of doing things. This tug of war, we know from our own experiences and the experiences of others, lasts a lifetime. Working with all this, however, does become a bit easier as you do it.

Probably, no one intends to construct schools and classrooms in a way that hurts the spirit of teachers or students. However, this happens unless we explicitly attend to the quality of relationships that are fostered. Hoffman (2009) points out that there is a relationship between social–emotional learning and academic learning but cautions educators not to conceive of caring in the classroom only as a tool for improving achievement. She notes a tendency for educators to think of emotions in the classroom as something that individuals "have" and that can be controlled, rather than thinking more holistically about the emotional context we create in classrooms and schools. Because relationships are a major part of that context, we examine teacher–student relationships, student–student relationships, and then discipline in what follows.

Student–Teacher Relationships

Establishing caring relationships with every student may be the most important thing a teacher can do to begin teaching to high achievement and closing the "achievement gap" (Bell, 2002–2003). A study in New Zealand establishes a direct link between "relationship-based pedagogy" and student academic learning. In a study looking into why so many Maori students (Maori are the indigenous people of New Zealand) did poorly in school and dropped out, Maori students spoke at length about the importance of their relationships with teachers. As secondary-level teachers were trained to develop personal relationships with their Maori students and to use interactive teaching strategies such as cooperative learning, the attendance and achievement of all their students, especially Maori students, began to improve (Bishop, Berryman, Cavanagh, & Teddy, 2009). In other words, strengthened teacher–student relationships lead to better student engagement in the classroom, which in turn leads to higher student achievement (Klem & Connell, 2004).

But, as with many educational concepts, there are different interpretations of what it means to care. Many beginning teachers use the words *care*, *love*, and *help* to express their reasons for entering the teaching profession. Look back at how you discussed loving and helping students [earlier]. What did your discussion suggest that you do to demonstrate care? What have you done [...] to act on your ideas?

Students experience teacher care through what the teacher does. Noddings (1995) explained that "caring is not just a warm, fuzzy feeling that makes people kind and likable … . When we care, we want to do our very best for the objects of our care." Gay (2010) elaborated on what caring and uncaring relationships look like: "Caring interpersonal relationships are characterized by patience, persistence, facilitation, validation, and empowerment for the participants. Uncaring ones are distinguished by impatience, intolerance, dictation, and control" (p. 49). Teachers usually find warm, constructive relationships easy to build with some students and much harder with other students.

Reflection 3.1 asks you to take a brief inventory of your reactions to different kinds of kids. The more honestly you face your present reactions, the better you can examine and work with them. As you do this exercise, keep in mind that the real problem in classrooms is not just how you feel about students. More significantly, it is about, on one hand, whether you allow negative feelings to persist and shape relationships with some students and, on the other hand, whether you allow positive feelings toward other kids to privilege them and give them access that the first group of students is not receiving.

[...] Which kinds of kids are you most likely to treat in ways that show patience, persistence, facilitation, validation, and empowerment? Which kinds of kids might you treat in ways that show impatience, intolerance, dictation, and control? Be bluntly honest here: now is the time to stand tall. Carl Grant recalls when Christine Sleeter pushed him to "stand tall" in developing his knowledge and interaction with students who have severe disabilities.

How you treat students affects how they regard you. Based on what you wrote in Reflection 3.1, which students will probably react to you in ways that make you feel

> **Reflection 3.1**
>
> **Reactions to different kinds of kids**
>
> Jot down brief descriptions of the kinds of kids who provoke the following feelings in you:
>
> Kids you find it easy to like:
>
> Kids you find it hard to like:
>
> Kids you are sorry for:
>
> Kids you feel threatened by:
>
> Kids you identify with:
>
> Kids you gravitate toward:
>
> Kids you feel inadequate around:
>
> Kids you probably do not even notice:

competent, warm, and respected? Think carefully here about how kids will react to *your treatment of them*. Although students bring into the classroom a wide range of personalities, feelings about school, problems, and prior experiences from their lives outside school, most of their reactions to you will stem from how you treat them. It is quite possible that students will "read" your feelings about them from your body language even before you have thought consciously about those feelings.

Student Dialogue 3.2

Gilbert: Now, this is a profound idea, and it makes me think about my fifth-grade teacher, old Mr. Franks. Poor Mr. Franks, I think he was just a little bit old and out of step, but we tormented him! We thought he was strange and slow to figure things out, so we did all kinds of things to upset him, like putting tacks on his chair, talking when he wanted us quiet, and hiding his things. He thought we were incorrigible, mostly because about half of us weren't White. We respected our other teachers, so we didn't act that way with them, but he brought out the worst in us.

Celia: And I bet the whole time he thought your behavior was a product of your home environment, right?

Gilbert: Bingo!

Lisa: You were mean to him just because he was old?

Gilbert: It wasn't … Not just because he was old, but he didn't seem to like us.

Lisa: Well, no wonder. I wouldn't like someone putting tacks on my chair, either.

Gilbert: But we tormented him *because* he didn't seem to like us. I guess our behavior made it worse. But if he would have started off by learning to say our names correctly, asking how our families were, or what we did over the weekend—anything to show an interest in us—I don't mean to suggest that if a teacher says, "Hello, Gilbert," I'm suddenly an angel. But most kids won't deliberately torment someone who seems to genuinely like them.

[...] By listening closely to [students], we can tune in to "the humanness of every child" and their capacities "to be creators, builders, and actors in their education and their lives" (Schultz, 2003, p. 35). We have found it very helpful as teachers to identify early on those students we find it difficult to relate to and intentionally try to get to know them personally. We do not suggest snooping into the student's private life or looking for problems the student may have but rather discovering what interests the student, what kind of person the student is trying to become, what hopes and dreams the student may have, and what the student is good at. Most students respond when a teacher shows a genuine interest in him or her as a person.

As Reflection 3.1 illustrates, "care" is expressed as action. Reflection 3.2 asks you to consider the kinds of actions that best express care. Circle those that help to describe what it means to act on care.

Discuss with your classmates which terms you selected and why. How many of your classmates selected most or all of them? Which were not selected? Did those terms

Reflection 3.2

What does it mean to care?

To nurture	To ensure students feel cared about	To engage in the whole life of students, both in and out of school
To keep students safe from harm	To work for social justice	To show concern for the well being of each individual
To work explicitly against racism	To prepare students for the kind of future you would want for your own children	To encourage students to be their best

that were not selected deal with social justice, or did they deal with the less provocative issues regarding care such as "encouraging students to be their best?" You may be puzzled why we included some terms above.

We did so because ironically students who may need the most caring schools tend to get the least, partly because of a widening cultural gap between teachers and students that plays out in various ways. One reflection of this gap is the fact that the great majority of teachers are White, whereas student populations are rapidly diversifying. It is quite common that young White teachers worry about being seen as racist. To appear accepting of everyone, they are often inadvertently simultaneously friendly but condescending toward students of color. This stance is manifest when the teacher allows students to get by without working very hard, allows them to get away with things, avoids talking with their parents, or believes their parents cannot be helpful in their education.

Student Dialogue 3.3

Lisa: Oh, no, I'm so embarrassed! I think I did that in my field experience classroom last term, and didn't realize it. I've never worked in a classroom that has a lot of minority kids in it, and, well, I was worried about whether I would be able to get along with them. I remember one day this Black girl was snatching a book away from a White kid, and I saw her but didn't say anything because I was so busy trying to make sure she liked me. I know that wasn't right, but I'm worried about not being racist.

Celia: I know you meant well, Lisa. But how will the little girl learn what's right and wrong if we don't teach her? You don't want to be cold when you are scolding someone; you can be kind and firm at the same time.

Gilbert: I think all of us worry about whether kids like us or not, it isn't just you. I do, too.

Celia: Yeah, I guess I do, too. I'm thinking now about my third-grade teacher Señora Baca. What was great about her was that I knew she believed I was smart and she cared about whether or not I learned. She was strict—you wouldn't dare snatch a book from another kid in her room. But not because she was mean; she wasn't mean. She treated us like we were smart, and you wouldn't want to disappoint someone who cares for you that much.

Gilbert: I think the problem is about learning not to think that being soft and being caring are the same things. Being soft really doesn't help kids. Being firm does help them. The hard thing is being firm consistently with everyone.

Another reflection of a cultural gap is the growing number of teacher–student relationships that cross some form of difference, including race, ethnicity, language, social class, or ability. Relationships are often thwarted when teachers leap to judgments about their students. Below, Marx and Pennington (2003) offer an example:

> The case of Rachel, a teacher candidate who described one child she met for just one 30-minute session as having an "apathetic attitude" toward English and education altogether. Crucial to her judgment was the fact that this child, Miguel, did not speak during their time together. In her journal, she wrote that, "I saw a child who was not proficient in even his native language, let alone in English" (Interview No. 4 with Rachel). Since she spoke no Spanish and, in their time together, neither did Miguel, there was no way for Rachel to know this.
>
> (p. 101)

We have worked with beginning teachers who assume that students do not receive love from homes affected by poverty and, therefore, see their job as giving love they believe the student is not receiving otherwise. Sometimes this assumption, which can be laced with pity, is based only on children's demands to be hugged in school. However, based on research into child neglect, Finzi, Ram, Har-Even, Shnit, and Weizman (2001) point out that children who are truly neglected are more likely to withdraw from adults than to seek affection from them. We have also worked with teachers who feel sorry for students with disabilities, describing them as "unfortunate." It is probably impossible to build supportive, authentic caring relationships on negative assumptions or pity.

It is also difficult to build respectful relationships on color blindness, because when one claims not to see color, one ignores much of a person's identity. Thompson (1998) reminds us that a predominantly White teaching force will need to be mindful of how they demonstrate care because,

> In contrast to most White feminist theories of care, Black feminist theories of care have paid close attention to the issue of race; and whereas color-blind theories of care tend to emphasize the innocence, Black feminist ethical theories emphasize knowledge.
>
> (p. 532)

In a study of a high school that serves mainly Mexican-American students, Valenzuela (1999) distinguished between two kinds of care: *aesthetic* and *authentic*. Aesthetic care attends to how students act or express themselves with respect to schooling. Teachers who assume an aesthetic stance toward care judge students on the basis of whether they adhere to the demands of the school and see care as something students earn. Teachers reward students who show interest in school and regard those who do not as "uncaring" and, therefore, deserving of teachers' low esteem. Authentic care, on the other hand, is based on a reciprocal relationship between teacher and student; building the relationship comes first. As an adult in relationship with young people, the teacher has a responsibility to know students as whole people and to nurture their development. Valenzuela points out that this relationship is especially important to Mexican-American students who grow up in communities in which *educación* forms the basis of their learning. The term *educación*, "refers to the family's role of inculcating in children a sense of moral, social, and personal responsibility and serves as the foundation for all other learning" (p. 23). The majority of the teachers in the high school she studied brought an aesthetic but not an authentic view of caring, insisting that students "buy in" to the assimilation function of schooling to earn teachers' care. The students, feeling uncared for at school, rejected schooling. Valenzuela argues that care must not subtract from students' important social and cultural resources, such as language. Authentic care encourages students to develop their language and culture, while at the same time, providing students with the opportunities and resources to develop academic skills and encouragement to strive for the best opportunities academically.

Student Dialogue 3.4

Gilbert: *Educación?* Celia, you speak Spanish, right? What are they talking about here?

Celia: Well, in my community, it's important to teach kids not just how to read and count, but also how to live right: how to be respectable and have good values, how to take care of themselves and other people.

Gilbert: Like, someone can be a well-educated idiot in real life, and that person wouldn't have *educación*?

Celia: Sort of like that. The thing that's important is that it's your responsibility to guide kids. You don't wait to see if they're interested. You're there for them, teaching them, helping them become good people. I grew up expecting that from adults. It didn't mean I was always good, but I expected adults to care enough about me personally to guide me. I think, Lisa, that is what it means to be firm and warm at the same time.

Lisa: I like that idea!

Lisa, Celia, and Gilbert all see *educación* as a powerful idea. An idea, we would have probably heard them say, if we could have listened in longer, that is not receiving its fair amount attention in schools, especially poor and urban schools.

Noddings (2005) sees care as an interpersonal relationship that rests not just on what a teacher does or feels but also on the extent to which students actually feel cared for. She points out that

> The relational view is hard for some American thinkers to accept because the Western tradition puts such great emphasis on individualism. In that tradition, it is almost instinctive to regard virtues as personal possessions, hard-won through a grueling process of character building.

Thus, the teacher who insists that his or her job is just to teach, or that students should simply ignore how the teacher feels about them, is rejecting the centrality of relationships, which many students find essential.

Gay (2010) claims,

> teachers who really care about students honor their humanity, hold them in high esteem, expect high performance from them, and use strategies to fulfill their expectations. They also model academic, social, personal, and moral behaviors and values for students to emulate. Students, in kind, feel obligated to be worthy of being so honored.
>
> (p. 48)

Feeling warm and sentimental toward students without translating care into acting on high expectations constitutes a form of "academic neglect" (p. 48), as does delivering content to students without building rapport. This is especially so with students for whom teacher–student rapport is essential to their learning.

Reflection 3.3 invites you to interview three people to find out how they view or remember their favorite teacher. The three people you interview can be of any age; try to select people from different backgrounds to get a range of views.

When you finish, examine the three descriptions for evidence of teacher care. Then reread the material above from the work of Valenzuela, Noddings, and Gay; circle any words or phrases that reflected what you heard in the interviews. What have you learned from this activity that you will act on the next time you are with students?

In research studies, students usually describe their favorite teachers as "caring" but not necessarily as nice all the time (Alder, 2002; Gay, 2010; Irvine, 2003). In general, students have more regard for "warm demanders" than for teachers who let them slide by (Kleinfeld, 1975). Warm demanders not only expect a good deal from students but also support students, so that they can achieve; warm demanders demonstrate that they like and respect their students as people. Did your interviews reveal favorite teachers who were both warm and demanding?

> **Reflection 3.3**
>
> **Favorite teachers**
>
> Ask three people to describe their favorite teacher to you, and why this teacher is or was the person's favorite. Write their descriptions below.
>
> Person 1:
>
> Person 2:
>
> Person 3:

Teachers may wonder how to demonstrate care for lesbian, gay, bisexual, or transgendered (LGBT) students in a way that acknowledges their identities or identity struggles, particularly if a student is wrestling with his or her own sexual identity. Teachers who include LGBT people and issues in curriculum and who actively support "safe schools" policies in their own schools demonstrate care for people of diverse gender identities. Such demonstrations of care signal to LGBT students that this is an understanding teacher one can talk with.

Caring teachers recognize the barriers that students face and help students to deal with them. Stereotypes are significant barriers faced by students of color, female students, LGBT students, and students who are disabled. When students grow up seeing people like themselves repeatedly portrayed as incapable, they come to doubt their own capability. African-American students come to feel this way about their ability to take standardized tests, for example; female students often feel this way about their ability to excel in science or technology. Steele and Aronson (1995) explain that

> The existence of a negative stereotype about a group to which one belongs ... means that in situations where the stereotype is applicable, one is at risk of confirming it as a self-characteristic, both to one's self and to others who know the stereotype.
>
> (p. 808)

Students perform worse than they would otherwise when placed in a situation in which they are afraid of "living down" to an expectation. Caring relationships are essential to help students get past this barrier. In an authentic caring relationship, a teacher demonstrates his or her belief in the student's capability by holding the student to high standards while supporting and encouraging the student along the way and showing respect for the student's home background.

Student Dialogue 3.5

Lisa: I've got an example. It's math. I grew up with this phobia thing about math, you know, like, girls aren't supposed to be good in math.

Celia: Me too.

Lisa: Yeah, and like, when we had to take big tests in math, I just froze. I got terrible scores. I had this geometry teacher who didn't help any; he pretty much ignored the girls in class. Then we would take a test and not do very well, and he'd say, see? What can you expect? Well, he didn't actually say that, but he'd look at us girls like we were just lame. And that seemed to make us lame.

Celia: It's even worse being a girl with a Spanish accent! I was so afraid that I'd let my family down, I think the stress alone froze my brain.

Student–Student Relationships

For several reasons, students' relationships with each other, in addition to their relationships with the teacher, are central to caring classrooms. Students learn better when they feel emotionally safe than when they do not. Students also can learn a great deal from the diverse perspectives of peers, if teachers create a foundation for peer learning. In addition, because democratic life is social, preparation for life in a democracy should encourage learning to respect and communicate with people who are different from oneself. A story from a classroom illustrates:

A middle-school teacher who teaches in a fairly diverse school believes passionately in democracy and strives to make her classroom one in which students get to know each other, develop respect for each other, and learn to discuss controversial issues. She told a story about what happened in her classroom right after 9/11/01:

> I was having a debate with my students about whether we should bomb Afghanistan. The majority of my students said, "No, we shouldn't, because we would be bombing innocent civilians, we would be doing what was done to us, it wouldn't solve anything, et cetera." But I had two boys who said, "Yeah, we just need to bomb them, look what they did to us, we just need to bomb them." And I let the kids talk, and all the different people tried to convince these boys that they didn't feel that this was right. Every day I try to create an atmosphere in the classroom where we can have this kind of discussion, where students feel free to disagree respectfully with one another as they explore their ideas. I'm not going to tell the students my

own personal opinions ... I want them to think for themselves. Finally one of the girls said, "Well, what about Ahmed? (Ahmed was a Pakistani student who disappeared two days after September 11. I think he went back to Pakistan.) And so the students asked, "What about Ahmed? He's over there. What will happen to him?" And those same two boys changed their minds and said, "Then we've got to come home. ... We shouldn't bomb them." No great arguments, no amount of rationale would change their minds, only the human connection they had with their friend Ahmed.

(Sleeter, 2005, pp. 173–174)

In this example, the teacher had built community among her students. She had enabled them to find common ground, develop empathy, and base decisions in empathy.

Building partnership relationships in the classroom helps students find common ground and build community with each other. Community and empathy do not come automatically, but they can be cultivated (Eisler, 2000). Empathy means being able to discriminate emotion in other people, take the role and perspective of another, and modulate one's own emotional expression as a result (Feshbach, 1975). Students need not necessarily agree with each other's viewpoints, but they can learn to appreciate that another student's viewpoint makes sense to him or her. They should, therefore, try to tune into how others feel about things they care deeply about (Feshbach & Feshbach, 1987).

As young people move from childhood through adolescence, they become increasingly preoccupied with identity and social relationships. Even very young children are busily constructing a sense of who they are, taking in clues from their social context. Van Ausdale and Feagin (2001) studied how children as young as 3 years old learned about race and racism in a day care center. Contrary to what some adults commonly believed, the children recognized differences in skin color. Although they had only begun to learn stereotypes associated with color in the wider society, the children used color to distinguish among themselves and as a marker of exclusion and inclusion. Children also had some awareness of race relations in the wider society in that the White children began to act out authority over children of color. Carl's grandson, while in day care, was excluded from attending a birthday party because of his skin color. The child having the party, who was a good classroom and playground buddy, told the author's grandson that he could not come to his party because he is "Black."

According to Gifford-Smith and Brownell (2003), by middle childhood, "children can truly be said to participate in a separate world of their peers" (p. 236); more than 30% of children's social interactions are with peers. Cliques and other groupings become more defined, and structure who interacts with whom, when, and about what. As this peer structure develops, some young people feel liked and supported whereas others feel rejected and left out. As you can probably recall from your own adolescence, groups compete against each other, sometimes through mild rivalry and other times violently. Bullying has recently become recognized as a serious problem in student–student relationships; in the United States, for example, almost one fifth of elementary students report having been bullied (Drake, Price, & Telljohann, 2003). Victims of bullying tend to achieve poorly; there is probably a circular relationship here, with low-achieving students being picked on, and the experience of being bullied leading many to avoid school (Swearer, Espelage, Vaillancourt, & Hymal, 2010). Bullying today takes place in ways not known in your mother's day. Students, Carl discovered during his recent observation in a school, send one another "I am going to get you after school" text messages on their cell phones.

By late elementary and middle school, societal, school, and peer contexts take a toll on the self-esteem of some groups of students more than others. These include disproportionately African-Americans boys (Madhere, 1991), Latina and White girls (U.S. Department of Education, 1998), and LGBT students, particularly transgender students (GLSEN Research Department, 2001). Like all young people, gay and lesbian students first experience erotic feelings around the age of 9, on the average. Unlike their heterosexual peers, however, by adolescence LGBT youth are struggling with feelings they have learned are considered socially unacceptable. [This] can take a huge toll on their self-esteem (Sears, 1993). Identity and self-esteem derive not just from peer interactions but also from images and treatment of oneself and people like oneself outside school.

Although peer groups can contribute to stereotyping and exclusion, the good news is that they can also counter negative images. For example, Tatum (1997) in her book, *Why Are All the Black Kids Sitting Together in the Cafeteria?*, emphasizes that forming social groups with peers "like oneself" facilitates the formation of a positive identity as well as a sense of belonging. At times, too, group formation serves to protect students whose identities are devalued by the school setting and curriculum. Recall your middle-school and high-school days. Your circle of friends was important, because they not only provided you with someone(s) to hang out with on the phone in the evening or go to the mall with on the weekend but also supported your self-concept, identity, and cultural values. Tatum stresses the need for appreciating the development of self-concept and engaging in conversations across currently existing racial and ethnic divides. For classroom teachers, the issue is not one of preventing peer group formations but rather of recognizing that children and youth bring into the classroom concern about who they are in relationship to peers and experiences working through these concerns. In the classroom, and in that context of peer formations, how can teachers promote development of respectful and caring relationships?

We can also look at relationships across the school, asking how circles of friends can be built that traverse differences. For example, Calabrese et al. (2008) reported a study of the impact of the Circle of Friends program, which seeks to build relationships between students inside and outside special education. Most attempts to do so take place in general education rather than special education classrooms, but some students with disabilities spend much of their time in special education. Circle of Friends involves pairing students with disabilities with peers without disabilities and then organizing activities for them to do together. The researchers found that for both parties—those with and those without disabilities—friendships gradually developed that often expanded to include more students. Over time, the circle of friends of the students with disabilities grew. At the same time, students without disabilities learned to see people with disabilities as people first with whom they had things in common. The researchers concluded that intentional plans to break down isolation and segregation, such as this program, can be transformative to all participants.

Student Dialogue 3.6

Gilbert: Man, I wish my teachers would have understood this. I was a good student. I was a great student, in fact. But the other kids thought I was weird. The Black kids thought I looked too Asian, and the Asian kids were prejudiced against Black kids, so I didn't fit anywhere. To their credit, my parents tried to encourage me to appreciate being biracial, but that didn't carry over into how kids saw me. High school was the worst because by then all of the guys were trying to see how many girls they could get. All of that just isn't me.

Lisa: I would have liked you back then, Gilbert!

Gilbert: No, you wouldn't have. Lisa, you're the kind who ends up being popular.

Lisa: I wasn't exactly popular. I mean, I liked sports all my life, and especially tennis. But I hated being called a tomboy. In sixth grade, these two boys who I thought were cute told me that no one would ever want to marry me because I was too much of a tomboy. Well, from then on, I made sure I was feminine. I got my hair styled, started paying attention to fashions, wearing a little makeup. OK, you're right, I did want to be popular, but I had to work at it, because I didn't want to give up sports in order to be accepted.

Celia: In elementary school, most of the other kids spoke English without an accent, and they weren't as dark as I am. I wanted to be White!

Lisa: You're kidding!

Celia: No, I'm not. I used to drink white milk all the time to try to be White. I loved chocolate milk, but I didn't drink it because I was afraid it would make me even browner than I already am. What was so hard, though, was that I loved spending summers in Guanajuato with my grandmother, and she is even darker than I am! I felt at home there. Then I'd come back to Los Angeles and go back to school. I really felt torn because the people I loved most looked like the kids who were most harassed in my school—the kids I tried not to look like. I got good at pretending it didn't hurt. But it did.

Operating in a test-crazed environment and dealing with the pressures encountered during a typical work day, teachers sometimes do not give our full attention to the reality that students are confronting challenges of self-identity, group identity, and the many other social factors that influence becoming the person they hope to become.

Discipline

Many teachers argue that discipline is the top prerequisite for good teaching and student learning. However, there are differences among discipline, classroom management, punishment, and authoritarianism. Understanding these differences is pertinent to good multicultural teaching and improving academic achievement. As you read the definitions later, ask yourself which approach suits your style of teaching.

Discipline deals with how children behave in the classroom and the teacher's ability to influence that behavior. Discipline is directed toward oneself; responsibility comes from within the person. It is ongoing and central to the learning process, especially during this time of stress over students' achievement. Discipline helps students assume responsibility for their behavior through introducing the ideas of dignity and respect for both self and others (Fuller, 2001).

Classroom management is broader in scope than discipline. It includes everything teachers do to increase student involvement and cooperation and to establish a healthy, caring, productive working environment for students. In addition, classroom management includes the orchestration of a classroom—planning curriculum, organizing procedures and resources, arranging the environment to maximize learning, monitoring student progress, and anticipating students' needs and problems (Lemlech, 1991). From a multicultural perspective, classroom management refers to the teacher's ability to arrange classroom learning, so that it welcomes and affirms all students, and it promotes cooperation and high expectations across ethnic, gender, and socioeconomic lines.

Punishment means paying or receiving a penalty for a deed or offense committed against a set of rules or authority. Students often perceive punishment in the classroom as an "us against them" situation—teacher against student. It usually indicates that someone in authority has the power to distribute the penalty. In schools, punishment may include the loss of privileges such as recess or consequences such as suspension or expulsion from school.

Authoritarianism is about control; teachers show students that the teacher is "boss." Sometimes teachers are unaware of the extent to which they are being authoritarian, attributing their behavior to tough love or giving students what they need. Furthermore, sometimes in culturally diverse classrooms, teachers misinterpret ordinary student behavior as bad or challenging the teacher's authority. Of course, teachers are the legal and professional authorities in the classroom, and that is as it should be. However, when teachers show students care and respect by providing an engaging curriculum placed in a context that acknowledges the students' background, authoritarianism can give way to self-discipline.

A few of our education students tell us that they had thought being a teacher meant they should "control" the class—be the figure of authority or boss. Many, perhaps the majority, say that they want to help their students develop self-discipline by providing good classroom management, and teaching them how to effectively relate to their peers. However, practically all of our students ask us what kind of discipline/classroom management we recommend. This query comes in the form of direct questions and what-if questions.

We try to provide you with some direction, but we caution teacher candidates that there are no surefire, one-answer methods. Helping students to build self-discipline generally requires knowing the students and the context of the situation. We ask teacher candidates to think of their three favorite teachers and to recall whether they all ran their classes the same way. Most come to the conclusion that there is no little bag of tricks to help them with classroom discipline. We believe, however, that developing a caring classroom goes a long way in helping everyone to be friendly and respectful of one another: teacher and students.

Teachers can do quite a lot to build caring classrooms and schools. Positive relationships that nurture identity and self-esteem do not just automatically happen. In the remainder of this [reading], we will develop three building blocks for teaching that provide a foundation for building caring classrooms and schools:

> **Building Block 6:** Using Conflict Resolution
> **Building Block 7:** Addressing Prejudice and Stereotyping
> **Building Block 8:** Using Cooperative Learning

Building Block 6: Using Conflict Resolution

Problems involving relationships are evident when there is conflict. The conflict might be a fight or an argument, a student talking back angrily, or a student snatching something away from someone else. As teachers we are often unprepared for conflict. We find it distressing because it upsets our emotional well-being, so we try to make it go away as quickly as possible. Discipline problems, for example, are often manifestations of relationship conflicts.

D'Ambra (2004) describes a spectrum of responses to conflict, in terms of the extent to which responses involve mutual participation in seeking a resolution. The responses include the following:

- Conflict suppression using force.
- Conflict management using force, adjudication, or arbitration. In a classroom, this would involve spelling out classroom rules and then applying them regularly and consistently.
- Conflict resolution, which involves negotiation to determine solutions to conflicts after they have arisen.
- Conflict prevention, which involves proactive negotiation and mediation to identify potential problems before they happen, and working out preventive solutions.
- Culture of dialogue, which involves assuming that differences always exist and need to be talked out to develop a respectful dialogue; which is not driven by problems but rather by compassion and the value of dialogue across differences.

Beginning teachers often resort to conflict suppression or conflict management, not anticipating conflict until it erupts. Reflection 3.4 asks you to recall an example of each of these responses to conflict in an education environment.

Reflection 3.4

Examples of responses to conflict

Think of an example of each response to conflict in an education environment:

Conflict suppression:

Conflict management:

Conflict resolution:

Conflict prevention:

Culture of dialogue:

Which responses to conflict were easiest to recall? Which were the most difficult? Because conflict is usually uncomfortable, unless we are prepared to react differently to it, we usually react either by force or by trying to manage it. This is true of teachers as well as students. Stopping or attempting to manage conflict by punishment is a common response to classroom discipline problems. Although conflict can usually be stopped through force or forceful management, these responses do not build an environment that works constructively with conflict. As Gathercoal (1993) observed, "Punishment leaves students hating and fearing educators. They respond by lying, cheating, withdrawing, and often becoming non-participants in school activities" (p. 17).

From a more proactive stance, conflict can be regarded as neither positive nor negative but rather as a meaningful part of human existence. Most of us are involved in conflicts every day. People have conflicts with themselves over what to eat, or whether to go home for spring break or to go to Florida with friends. At home, school, or on the playground, conflicts often provide wonderful opportunities to learn that people's opinions can differ on almost any issue, and sometimes we need to rethink our own perspective based on encountering someone else's. Conflicts also provide opportunities to learn self-discipline, respect for others, respect for self, respect for the laws of society, and respect for diversity. The outcome from conflict may be negative or positive depending on the actions taken by the parties involved.

Because conflict resolution is so important to build caring classrooms with respectful relationships, conflict resolution programs have gradually become increasingly important. The first conflict resolution programs in schools emerged in the early 1970s, "sparked by the increasing concern of educators and parents about violence in the schools" (Girard & Koch, 1996, p. 111). Growing out of these earlier efforts, the National Association for Mediation in Education was established in 1984. The organization changed its name to the National Institute for Dispute Resolution, and it works toward the development and implementation of conflict resolution and peer mediation programs in the schools.

Many schools today dedicate a great deal of time and attention to conflict resolution and the elimination of violence. Some states, such as Wisconsin, require that prospective teachers receive training in conflict resolution. Some states have programs where students can obtain an advanced degree in conflict resolution. Some school districts advocate teaching conflict resolution as early as kindergarten and the primary grades, so that children will be able to resolve conflicts such as playground disputes over balls and use of swings and classroom conflict over pencils, computers, and friendships.

Conflict resolution programs can be quite extensive; reviewing them or showing you how to implement them is beyond the scope of this [reading]. As Cirillo et al. (1998) point out, although no single program is a cure-all, when students are taught alternatives to violence, they have been found less likely to engage in violent behavior. In the next few pages, we will help you get started by showing alternatives.

One of the first steps in resolving conflict is to explain to students three common ways that conflict is handled, guiding them to think through which way is most productive and why. Table 3.1 presents three different ways to deal with conflict.

You can present these alternatives to students and ask which they see as preferable, and which method they believe that their parents would like them to use in conflict resolution.

TABLE 3.1 Three Ways to Deal With Conflict: Which Do You Think Teachers Recommend?

Denial: When someone is angry from a conflict, instead of saying he or she is angry, the person denies that anything is wrong. This does not allow for a resolution of the conflict because the second person does not know what is wrong or why the first person may be angry. If the situation is not addressed, it can happen again.

Confrontation: When one or more students verbally or physically attack another student or students. The attack usually happens when the parties are not willing to listen to each other's side of the problem or to discuss it. Instead they attack the other person or her or his ideas.

Problem solving: When the students work to resolve their difficulty. Each person listens to the other and looks for ways that their problem may be amicably resolved.

The problem-solving approach is the one that teachers recommend and teach children. Although this choice seems obvious, children do not automatically know how to make it work. To make it work, young students can learn skills such as communication skills, negotiation, mediation, apologizing, postponing gratification, and compromising. We discuss two essential communication skills: "I messages" and active listening as follows.

I Messages and Active Listening

The use of I messages can be important for maintaining good student–teacher rapport and avoiding more severe conflict. There is no ducking the issue: I messages get rid of "he said, she said" accusations and locate the speaking and feelings of the parties at a personal level.

Reflection 3.5 allows you to practice the three parts of I messages: (1) state how you feel, (2) state the other person's behavior that prompts that feeling, and (3) state what you would like the other person to do. Notice that I messages do not lay blame on the other person or make value judgments about her or his behavior. Rather, they ask the other person to change behavior that is creating uncomfortable feelings for the speaker. To practice an I message, pretend that you are in a classroom and find out that a student told his former teacher that you are mean to him and pick on him every day. Write an I message that would let the student know how you feel about this.

How difficult was it to phrase your concern as an I message rather than as an accusation? I messages feel awkward at first, and they do not come automatically when we are feeling upset. You can have students role-play creating I messages, so they get used to how they are stated, how they sound, and how they make each person feel.

> ### Reflection 3.5
>
> #### Practice using I messages
>
> I feel (name the feeling):
>
> When you (describe the behavior):
>
> I want (tell what would make the situation better for you):

Active listening is a useful skill that complements I messages. Active listening means attending closely to what the other person is saying—actually hearing not just the words but also the message behind the words. Often in a conflict situation, we are so busy trying to get our own point of view across that we do not hear the other person's viewpoint very well. Think back to a recent conflict you had with someone. Once you get the example in your mind, rewind your mind's tape recorder. Then play it back and assess your own behavior.

Evaluate your behavior with respect to the active listening skills below, which are recommended in Sunburst Communication's (1994) *Student Workshop: Conflict Resolution Skills*:

- Show that you are interested
- Ask questions if there is something you do not understand
- Listen for the feeling of the speaker
- Do not interrupt, change the subject or make up your mind before the person finishes speaking

Which active listening behaviors did you use? Which did you fail to use?

With practice, students can develop skill in active listening. Role-playing is a useful way to offer this practice. Some teachers also make creative use of puppets or theater in the classroom, inviting students to act out conflicts, disputes, and disagreements they see around them, using I messages and active listening.

Conflict Resolution Approaches

Conflict resolution skills help students get along with one another and deal with the different people and perspectives they encounter. In addition, conflict resolution can limit the extent to which students become emotionally upset. Most models for resolving conflict recommend similar procedures. Tables 3.2 and 3.3 illustrate two models. Table 3.2 shows recommendations from Sunburst Communication (1994). Table 3.3 shows steps in the Framework for Collaborative Negotiation proposed by Raider and Coleman (1992).

Reflection 3.6 asks you to compare the models in Tables 3.2 and 3.3 and identify their similarities. After listing their similarities, note where I messages fit in as a way of expressing feelings and where active listening fits in as a way of hearing feelings.

TABLE 3.2 **Conflict Resolution Procedures**

1. Find a good time and place to talk.
2. Discuss the problem.
   Get the facts.
   Use active listening—show interest, ask questions, pay attention, and repeat to make sure you have it right.
   Use I messages to say how you feel.
   Focus on the problem, not the person.
   Avoid communication blockers.
3. Brainstorm for solutions.
   Be willing to compromise. Give a little to get a little.
4. Choose a solution that works for everybody.
5. Try the solution.
   If the solution does not work: go back to step 3.

Source: Sunburst Communication (1994)

TABLE 3.3 **Framework for Collaborative Negotiation**

Stages	*Tasks (Examples)*
Planning	Decide if the conflict is negotiable. Separate needs from positions. Try to see the other side's point of view.
Creating climate for negotiating	Establish trust and rapport.
Informing and questioning	Use "I" statements and inform the other side as to your needs. Ask about the other side's needs.
Finding common ground	Identify problems that affect both sides. Try to consider the issues in terms of shared needs.
Brainstorming	Freely suggest ideas for solving the problem. Withhold judgment.
Choosing solution	Narrow down suggestions for solutions to the most promising ones for a lasting resolution.

Now that you have a sense of how to build communication skills and strategies for conflict resolution in the classroom, let us look at a common format for working out problems: class meetings.

> **Reflection 3.6**
>
> Similarities in conflict resolution frameworks

Class Meetings

Class meetings can be a powerful tool for resolving interpersonal conflicts and settling down the students, as well as addressing management and curriculum issues. The focus of any given meeting can vary widely, from a student seeking input on a personal issue to decisions regarding classroom policies. But class meetings are only truly effective when they involve genuine dialogue and include students' concerns, ideas, and voices. If the students are to take the process seriously, their voices should be at the heart of problem identification, discussion, and evaluation.

Class meetings are most effective when they occur frequently enough to serve as a negotiation tool, yet not so frequently that they become trivialized. They function best as one component of a democratic classroom in which opportunities for student input and idea sharing are continually sought and valued. The time taken to facilitate such ongoing discussion is repaid in student engagement and empowerment and students feeling emotionally secure and safe.

Students should help to form the class meeting structure; the following components are essential:

- A way for students to identify and submit meaningful problems for group discussion.
- A regular time set aside for the meeting process, and arrangement of classroom space to accommodate face-to-face discussion (a group circle is ideal).
- Guidelines to help students establish effective communication, such as refraining from using other students' names in problem description and using a means for equitable turn taking.
- An effective means of evaluation that includes finding out from the individual or group who brought a problem as to whether they feel that the solutions or advices are helpful. A brief follow-up discussion at the beginning of the next meeting might allow students to assess the quality of help given over time.

Student Dialogue 3.7

Gilbert: So part of our responsibility as teachers is to teach our students how to relate with each other? When I first thought about going into teaching, I thought mainly about teaching subjects, like history and reading. I enjoy working with kids but, to be honest, hadn't seen teaching things like I messages and active listening to be part of my curriculum.

Celia: Don't you think it would be worth it, though, in the long run? Think of all the aggravation you might head off before it happens!

Lisa: I like the idea, but need more information.

Gilbert's conception of teaching is held by many teacher candidates. There is so much more to teaching than covering the curriculum and transmitting information from one age group to the next age group. One of the roles of the teacher is teaching students how to get along with other students in ways that promote and respect one's voice and locus of control. Gilbert will have to modify his view as soon as possible, or he will place both himself and his students at an academic and social disadvantage.

A variety of materials that deal with conflict resolution are available. Increasingly, you can locate materials, organizations, and descriptions of program on the Internet. For Reflection 3.7, identify four websites that appear useful to you and write a brief description of them.

Reflection 3.7

Websites about conflict resolution

Using an Internet search engine, locate four websites that appear useful to you. For each, write the URL, the name of the website, and a brief description.

1.

2.

3.

4.

This activity is one that some students will blow off, saying, "I can do this one later." But if you do so, you will miss both the intended and unintended learning that comes with completing such an activity. Most of the time when we go to the Web, we are surprised by the additional resources and ideas we discover. *So go to the Web, good ideas await you.*

Most teachers strive to be a neutral or fair party in the classroom, especially when it comes to political, religious issues, and many social issues. [... A]ll teachers bring their baggage with them into the classroom. Teachers are influenced by their race or ethnicity, gender, sexuality, socioeconomic status, and religion. Any of these characteristics and their influence on one's everyday behavior, when not accepted by students or colleagues, can lead to conflict. G. Valentine (1997) suggests that to avoid such conflicts people need to have a clear understanding of their cultural perspectives, and how they influence attitudes and behavior. Understanding your own baggage, and helping students to realize that they too bring baggage with them, is critical in learning to work constructively with classroom conflict.

Building Block 7: Addressing Prejudice and Stereotyping

Students bring into the classroom perceptions about people through which they filter their understandings of everyone else. Classrooms themselves provide intense spaces for observing, interpreting, and reacting to different people. Describing an elementary classroom, Gallas (1998) observed,

> What had once seemed routine and mundane was, in fact, peculiar. It was peculiar that, for the purposes of education, twenty or more children, all of the same age, would be confined for several hours a day in a room with a woman as their sole caretaker.
>
> (p. 25)

She saw students' behavior in that environment as shaped by their gendered perceptions of their teacher, as well as by other categories through which they interpreted each other. After an extensive analysis of gendered behavior of primary-grade students, she concluded that "I cannot orchestrate what ought to be when I do not understand what is" (p. 140). By this, she meant that we cannot change how young people perceive themselves and each other without first understanding what they perceive and why. This requires careful observation and attentive listening.

Reflection 3.8 offers a way to begin to tune in to perceptions young people bring into the classroom about categories of people. When our teacher education students have tried this reflection, they have found surprises; see if you do, too. First, select a sociocultural group you feel is often stereotyped. Some of our students have selected categories like "American Indians," "Black women," "Muslims," "White U.S. males" "gay and lesbian people," "Spanish-speaking people," or "people in wheelchairs." Then, find out as much as you can about how young people conceptualize the group, and how the group is portrayed in society. Interview about five young people to find out what they believe they know about the group. Simply ask them to describe the group, and where they remember learning about it.

Then, gather additional data about how the group is represented in various dimensions of society. For example, you might look at the following:

- Media that children or youth of that age consume: What images of that group are shown, if any at all? (You might select a TV cartoon show, a TV situation comedy, or a movie.)
- School materials, such as textbooks: What images, if any, are shown?
- Religious institutions young people attend: How is this group represented in this context?

Reflection 3.8

Depictions of a group

Group you are investigating:

How young people described the group:

Where they learned their perceptions:

How the group is depicted by:

Media:

Textbooks:

Other:

From this investigation, to what extent did you find young people rely on stereotypes? Where does it appear they get their information? To what extent did their perspectives reflect images in popular media, such as TV or movies? To what extent did textbooks or other school materials replicate those images? Were you surprised by anything you found out?

Young people's awareness of human differences starts around the age of 3. Subsequently, they learn the social significance of differences from adults, media, schools, role models, religious institutions, and the like. Young people then act on what they have learned. To illustrate this idea, we interviewed Yer Thao, a Hmong man who had immigrated to the United States as a child. He described how other children treated him when he arrived in America as follows:

> We settled in a very poor area where we were mixed with Caucasians and African Americans, and we were the only Hmong family living in that area … We had neighbors [harassing us] like, they'd throw eggs at our door, they'd come and break our stuff, they threatened us. And it's like, they don't know who we are. My parents had to tell me, you go to school and you help us deal with this issue. But when you're out there, they call you names—You moved from the war and you are trying to find safety, but then you live in this country and you're living in fear. The people out there, they don't know who you are and you don't know who they are, and the way they react to you is very violent, and you feel like they could come and do anything to you at any time. And that is the most difficult part that I have been through … During lunch hours, or before school or after school you run into some students who were giving very hurtful behavior toward you because you are a bit different and you have to deal with those issues. If you are in trouble, and you don't speak the language, most of the time the teachers or the principal don't know how to solve your problems. Most of the time incidents are happening in the hallway and no teachers see it, the majority will say, well this guy, we don't know what he's saying. So it wasn't your fault but you tend to be the one accused as the person who starts all the problems.
>
> (Sleeter, 2001, Immigrant Kids, p. 2)

Very likely many of the perpetrators were not intentionally trying to hurt him, and his teachers believed that they cared about him. But at the same time, he looked "different," and initially spoke little English. Other students did not know how to interpret him, except through stereotypes of Asians, immigrants, and non-English speakers, which abound. Children in his school knew they could taunt him and blame problems on him, and get away with it, so they did.

Student Dialogue 3.8

Lisa: What do you guys think about kids calling each other "fag?" I hear that a lot in my field placement school, and no one does anything about it.

Gilbert: That word is like a punch in the stomach to me. Kids need to know it's wrong.

Lisa: But little kids, they don't know about homosexuality, they're just repeating what they hear. I always figured they'd outgrow it.

Gilbert: Outgrow it? Outgrow gay bashing? Look around you! If we don't teach kids, they'll model after what they hear and see.

Lisa: OK, but don't you think parents would get after you for teaching about gay issues?

Celia: I think you have two things going on here. One is whether to teach about gay issues as part of the curriculum. I think we'll get to that [later]. But right now, if we are talking about creating caring classrooms where kids feel safe, we need to stop derogatory name calling. Period. Like Gilbert said, even if a kid doesn't understand what "fag" means, if throwing the name at someone is like throwing a rock at that person, it needs to stop.

Kids at a very early age learn to do things in ways that will minimize their getting caught. This skill, you probably remember from your own growing up, becomes more sophisticated with age. Teachers have to be mindful about the quality of attention the new student, as well as the student who is gay or lesbian, receives. It is naïve to carry on as if mean-spiritedness among students will not take place—ignoring it can jeopardize the academic and social environment of the classroom.

Race, gender, physical size, and disability are markers of difference that play out in schools, as early as preschool. On the basis of an analysis of children's perceptions of race, for example, A. E. Lewis (2003) describes what she calls ascriptive processes through which markers of different identities are assigned to people through everyday interpersonal interactions.

> These ascriptive processes work primarily through interpersonal interactions in which we attempt to assess what we know about another person, first through the instantaneous reading or interpreting of available clues (e.g., visible cues such as skin color or facial features, auditory cues such as accent, spatial cues such as neighborhood), and second through rereading or reinterpreting initial assumptions as additional information becomes available. These processes operate in a largely relational manner: some people are determined to be the "same" (or "like me") and others are determined to be "different."
>
> (p. 151)

Young children ask questions freely before they learn that some kinds of questions are considered impolite. Adults often treat questions about human differences as rude, so children stop asking them. For example, we have seen parents become embarrassed and quickly hush a child who innocently asks a question about race or disability. From such actions, children become bewildered about how they should handle their curiosities. Many respond by learning that such questions are taboo. They then base their ideas on what they hear from family and friends or encounter in the media. Often young people learn to verbalize feelings about differences in the form of jokes, snide remarks, and name calling.

Left unaddressed, students' interpretations of and attitudes toward peers who differ from themselves can degenerate into harassment and sometimes violence. According to Juvonen (2001), about one quarter of U.S. students "repeatedly either engage in or are the targets of bullying tactics that contribute to the climate of fear." Furthermore, "children who view themselves as targets of bullying show high levels of anxiety and depression that impede their school performance." Harassment and bullying can escalate from name calling into physical violence. Educators who do nothing about it not only fail to teach young people how to live civilly together but may also risk a lawsuit (Zirkel, 2003).

Caring teachers can begin to address stereotyping, prejudice, and harassment using a four-pronged approach: (1) raising awareness of stereotyping, (2) teaching about what prejudice and discrimination are, (3) taking a stand against hurting people, and (4) helping young people learn to prevent or challenge discrimination.

Raising Awareness of Stereotyping

To begin raising awareness of prejudice and stereotyping, an elementary teacher we know taught her students to become "stereotype detectives," starting with stereotypes of American-Indians. First, she asked students to draw a picture of American-Indians. Then she read a children's book about American-Indians, taking care to select one that is recommended by American-Indians themselves (Slapin & Seale, 1998). The book had vivid illustrations of people who differed from each other, and as her students listened to the story and viewed the illustrations, they realized that their drawings were limited. After reading the book, she had students compare representations in the book with their drawings and used this discussion to teach them what a "stereotype" is. She then took her students to the library, where they examined books to uncover stereotypes of American-Indians. She continued to contrast the stereotypes with factual information, over the course of an extensive unit in social studies and literature (Sleeter, 2001, Rethinking Indigenous People). By the end of the unit, the students knew what stereotypes are and how they limit perceptions, and they knew a good deal more than they had about indigenous Americans.

TABLE 3.4 Sample Websites Created by Specific Sociocultural Groups

Group	URL	Name of Website
Indigenous people	http://www.nativeweb.org/	Native Web
Black women	http://www.bcw.org/	Black Career Women
Muslims	http://www.amcnational.org/	American Muslim Council
Gay and lesbian people	http://www.glsen.org/	Gay, Lesbian, and Straight Education Network
People in wheelchairs	http://www.wheelchairnet.org/	Wheelchair Net

The process she used helped students to contrast what they thought were accurate conceptions of American-Indians, with Indian representations of themselves. A problem with stereotypes is that we assume them to be true unless we have alternative information with which to contrast the stereotype. Aiello (1979) described teaching about disabilities by bringing to class guest speakers who had disabilities. In one example, children asked a blind visitor whether she could cook. She explained that she put Braille labels on foods in her kitchen and that one of her favorite things to cook was spaghetti. A 7-year-old child, after meeting her, exclaimed, "What a relief. I thought handicapped people cried all day!" (p. 30).

As children got to know people personally, they discovered that in addition to being different from each other, we are also alike in many ways. Derman-Sparks (1989) recommends that teachers introduce a variety of differences—cultural, physical, and gendered—that students actually see and experience, here and now. Rather than treating differences as exotic, treat them as normal, intentionally helping students to recognize when they are basing their ideas about people on stereotypes.

In addition to dispelling stereotypes by meeting people, students can also find out how a group might define itself by locating websites created by members of specific groups. For example, through a search, we identified websites produced by organizations of people who are often stereotyped. Table 3.4 above illustrates what we found.

Students might browse websites that are appropriate to their age level, comparing representations with images they thought were accurate. As students develop an idea of differences between stereotyped images and more authentic representations, they can notice, seek out, and critique stereotyped images. At the same time, they begin to develop a more accurate basis for forming personal relationships with people whom they see as different from themselves.

Teach Directly About Prejudice and Discrimination

Teaching young people directly about prejudice and discrimination will give them language and conceptual tools to examine their school, community, and societal context and to talk about forms of prejudice and discrimination that they experience. Recently, we showed a videotaped session of a teacher teaching elementary children about discrimination. The audience consisted of other teachers and teacher candidates. The teacher in the videotape began explaining what discrimination is with reference to examples of sex discrimination that the children could relate to. She then went on to forms of discrimination that the children did not see as obvious, such as discrimination against immigrants based on accent or language. In the course of this discussion, she asked children what they thought may or may not occur that day. Teachers in the audience were struck that she was able to teach such a lesson and that the children were able to discuss it in meaningful terms.

Like the teacher in the videotape, you can define prejudice and discrimination using examples your students are able to understand. Let us examine some definitions written for adults that can guide your construction of definitions to use with young people.

Table 3.5 [...] includes four definitions and descriptions of discrimination. Study them and then, in Reflection 3.9, write a child-appropriate definition of discrimination that synthesizes key components in these definitions.

Reflection 3.9

Definition of discrimination

Keep on thinking! Several books and classroom resources are available to help teachers in teaching children and youth about prejudice and discrimination. Teaching Tolerance (http://www.tolerance.org/) is an excellent place to start; this website and magazine offers practical suggestions in addition to articles that can deepen your understanding of various forms of discrimination and how children see and experience it.

Below are ideas for learning and reflection in the classroom.

- Even young children have commonsense understandings of what is fair and unfair. Children's sense of fairness provides a launch pad for expanding their awareness. For example, kindergarten children might agree that everyone has a right to a snack at snack time and that it would be discriminatory to deny some students a snack.

- Historically, groups have fought and worked hard to make various forms of discrimination illegal. Learning about this history of struggle can help young people gain a deeper sense of the issues themselves, as well as how to bring about social change. You can find examples of how to teach about such struggles in books such as *Turning on Learning* (Grant & Sleeter, 2007) or the newspaper *Rethinking Schools* (http://www.rethinkingschools.org/).
- As reflected in the definition of the NASP, prejudice, discrimination, and racism are related but not the same. Students can examine how these concepts differ. Students can also apply this examination to construct definitions of sexism, heterosexism, and so forth.
- Some definitions suggest indicators of discrimination. Help students figure out indicators of discrimination in their own environment, such as on the playground or in how discipline is handled. Indicators can then be used to determine whether discrimination exists.
- At the same time, disputes arise because different people use and judge indicators differently and bring different experiences and values to bear on them. Furthermore, people disagree about what is fair for both the society as a whole and for individuals and groups within that society. Creating a fair society is a process that is never finished; grappling with issues of fairness and discrimination is a way to learn to engage productively in that process. Take, for example, the matter of snacks at snack time. Is it discriminatory to serve snacks that some children do not like? What about snacks that some cannot eat (such as milk for children who are lactose intolerant, which is quite common, especially among children who are not of European descent)? Talking through how to balance individual and group rights in the real world helps young people learn to think through what "fairness" means.

Take a Stand Against Hurting People

Henning-Stout, James, and MacIntosh (2000) argue that efforts to reduce harassment must have two immediate goals: "to increase safety for all children and youth, and to counter the heterosexism too often seen in school and community cultures" (p. 188). These goals were evident in programs that were effective in reducing harassment based on sexual orientation. Although Henning-Stout et al. examined schoolwide programs, their research offers insights that are useful at the classroom level for all kinds of harassment.

Think back to when you were in school. Do you remember teasing or name calling among children? (If you cannot remember back that far, ask a young person who is in school right now to help you out on this task.) Reflection 3.10 asks you to identify

TABLE 3.5　Definitions of Discrimination

National Institute of Environmental Health Sciences and National Institutes of Health

Discrimination is defined in civil rights law as unfavorable or unfair treatment of a person or class of persons in comparison to others who are not members of the protected class because of race, sex, color, religion, national origin, age, physical/mental handicap, sexual harassment, sexual orientation, or reprisal for opposition to discriminatory practices or participation in the Equal Employment Opportunity (EEO) process.

Federal EEO laws prohibit an employer from discriminating against persons in all aspects of employment, including recruitment, selection, evaluation, promotion, training, compensation, discipline, retention, and working conditions, because of their protected status.

http://www.niehs.nih.gov/oeeo/disc-def.htm

Law Office.com, West Legal Dictionary

Sex discrimination: Women and girls have long been excluded from many sports. In the 1970s, Congress passed Title IX of the 1972 Education Amendments (20 U.S.C.A. §§ 1681–1688 [1994]) to ban sex discrimination in publicly funded educational programs. After a round of litigation, followed by legislative amendments, a presidential veto, and a congressional override of the veto, Title IX was modified to give women and girls equal access to sports programs in schools that receive any measure of federal funding.

Under Title IX, schools must provide athletic opportunities to females that are proportionate to those provided to males. Courts do not require that complete equality occur overnight. Most courts engage in a three-pronged analysis to determine whether a school is fulfilling its obligations. First, the court examines whether athletic participation opportunities are provided to each sex in numbers substantially proportionate to their enrollment. If a school does not provide substantially proportionate participation opportunities, the court then determines whether the school can demonstrate a history of expanding the athletic programs for the underrepresented sex. If the school cannot so demonstrate, the court then asks whether the interests and abilities of the underrepresented sex have been accommodated by the school. If the court finds that the school has not accommodated student-athletes of the underrepresented sex, it may rule that the school is in violation of Title IX and order the school to take affirmative steps toward more equal treatment between the sexes.

Traditionally, courts have differentiated between contact and noncontact sports in determining a female's right to participation. A school may refrain from offering a contact sport for females if the reasoning is not based on an archaic, paternalistic, overbroad view of women. Courts are hesitant to mandate the creation of new teams, but most have no problem ordering that qualified females be allowed to play on exclusively male teams.

http://law.jrank.org/pages/10437/Sports-Law-Sex-Discrimination.html

Board of Public Education of the School District of Pittsburgh

The Board of Public Education of the School District of Pittsburgh requires that the School District maintain, at all times, an environment in which all stakeholders display and receive respect, tolerance, and civility. Stakeholders include … all employees, students, families of students, residents and all entities interacting, or doing business with the School District in any capacity … The Board considers human relations in the work and educational environment

(Continued)

TABLE 3.5 *Continued*

necessary to afford all stakeholders an opportunity to achieve optimal performance in a nondiscriminatory atmosphere. Therefore, the Board reaffirms its policy precluding invidious discrimination on the basis of race, gender, religion, age, national origin, disability, sexual orientation, or socioeconomic background. Human relationship is defined prescriptively and proscriptively as follows:

Human relationships are mutual respect, tolerance, and civility among all stakeholders.

Conduct reflecting human relationships will result in equity for all stakeholders regardless of race, gender, religion, age, national origin, disability, sexual orientation, or socioeconomic background.

Human relationships preclude invidious discrimination on the basis of race, gender, religion, age, national origin, disability, sexual orientation or socioeconomic background.

Human relationships preclude conduct, including language, overt, and covert actions, which may create or contribute to a hostile environment based on race, gender, religion, age, national origin, disability, sexual orientation, or socioeconomic background.

Human relationships preclude overt and covert exclusionary behavior that limits access to school activities and curricula based on race, gender, religion, age, national origin, disability, sexual orientation, or socioeconomic background.

http://www.pps.k12.pa.us/143110127104380/blank/browse.asp?a=383&BMDRN=2000&BCOB=0&c=56730

The National Association of School Psychologists (NASP) Position Statement on Racism, Prejudice, and Discrimination

The NASP is committed to promote the rights, welfare, educational, and mental health needs of all students. This can only be accomplished in a society that ensures that all people, including children and youth, are treated equitably without reference to race or ethnicity. NASP believes that racism, prejudice, and discrimination are harmful to children and youth because they can have a profoundly negative impact on school achievement, self-esteem, personal growth, and ultimately the welfare of all American society. A discussion of multicultural issues requires a definition of terms.

Prejudice: Prejudice is an attitude, opinion, or feeling formed without prior knowledge, thought, or reason.

Discrimination: Discrimination is differential treatment that favors one individual, group, or object over another. The source of discrimination is prejudice, and the actions are not systematized. Two forms of discrimination exist: *de jure*, which is discrimination based on state policy and *de facto*, which is discrimination, for example, in school based on housing patterns or the attitudes of people instead of state policy.

Racism: Racism is racial prejudice and discrimination supported by institutional power and authority used to the advantage of one race and the disadvantage of other race(s). The critical element of racism, which differentiates racism from prejudice and discrimination, is the use of institutional power and authority to support prejudice and enforce discriminatory behaviors in systematic ways with far reaching outcomes and effects.

http://www.nasponline.org/about_nasp/pospaper_rpd.aspx

> **Reflection 3.10**
>
> Harassment and teacher intervention
>
> Instances of teaching, name calling, or other harassment
>
> Things teachers did about it

specific instances of teasing, name calling, or other forms of harassment and everything a teacher did to intervene.

What kind of harassment did you recall? Where did it occur? What effect did it have on students? What would you have liked teachers to do?

Often our teacher education students tell us that some teachers do not intervene when kids tease each other or put each other down. The teachers chalk it up to kids being kids, or if the teasing seems mild and not moving toward physical confrontation, they give students space to work it out on their own. We know that usually teachers are not aware of teasing or name calling because kids do it largely when teachers are not around. To what extent is your experience similar?

When we have asked children and youth what they think teachers should do, overwhelmingly they say that teachers should tell children to stop. However, saying "stop" is not enough. Teachers should publicly take a stand on matters that involve hurting other people. Teachers are role models, and when they do not take a stand, children assume that they condone hurtful behavior. It makes a difference when we teach children that hurtful behaviors and name calling are mean and destructive. Often children do not understand the extent of the impact of their actions on another person.

What names have you been called that were hurtful? Are they names that you would share with a peer, or names that you are embarrassed to repeat? The saying "Sticks and stones will break my bones, but names will never hurt me" is useful because it can serve as the first line of defense in a situation that has the potential to escalate. However, names do hurt, and as teachers it is our responsibility to get that across to all students. Students need to learn that names are not the only things that can hurt. Ignoring someone, taking someone's possessions without asking, and yelling at someone are other examples of hurtful behavior. Children need to know that a given name or behavior may not hurt them personally but can still hurt someone else.

In a classroom, it is possible to generate a list of names and behaviors that students find mean-spirited and hurtful. Some teachers do this through open discussion, others ask children to anonymously write down names and behaviors that hurt; the teacher then compiles a list for public discussion. Explaining what those names really mean and why name calling is hurtful sends a message that certain behaviors are not condoned, and calling students certain names will not be tolerated. In addition, it makes the topic "concern and care for each other" a part of the normal classroom discourse.

Student Dialogue 3.9

Celia: I understand that we need to teach kids not to say derogatory things about each other, but won't verbalizing bad names give them ideas? What if they never thought about this until I bring it up in the classroom? Don't you think some kids will wait until the teacher is out of earshot and then start throwing some of these new words around?

Gilbert: I would have thought that until I watched a teacher work with this idea last term. She had the kids write down hurtful names, and then they talked about why the names hurt. She tried to get them to tune into what it feels like when you hurt. Then she did this little ceremony. She put the trashcan in the middle of the room, then one by one, the kids ripped up the paper where they had written the names they'd been called, and threw the pieces into the trash. Then the whole class took the trashcan out of the room and slammed the door. The teacher announced that these names would never again appear in the classroom. And as long as I was there, they didn't appear again.

Lisa: Wow, so she actually got them involved in stopping name calling. She brought peer pressure to bear on it. After a ceremony like that, the rest of the class will come down on someone who verbally hurts someone else!

A complicated issue is that of members of a racial or ethnic group calling one another derogatory names as a greeting and when in conversation with each other, where use of the term by anyone outside the group could lead to conflict. Although a teacher cannot control the names students use to communicate to one another outside of school, he or she can let all students know that such terminology is off limits inside school, regardless of whether it is used as a term of endearment or in a mean-spirited way. In addition, a teacher should let students know that (re)appropriating a term that has a long history of debasement is difficult and perhaps not the best investment of their time.

As issues involving fairness and justice become more controversial, teachers often wonder if they should take a stand or attempt to remain neutral. For example, will knowing that a teacher supports gay rights keep students from honestly discussing their own feelings and questions about sexual orientation? Teachers are in a position of power in the classroom, so many students are unsure whether they can actually disagree with teachers. In our own teaching, both of us let students know our stand on issues but at the same time encourage students to take their own stands. Debating and acknowledging different points of view are as old as the U.S. Constitution, and in caring classrooms, people can participate. Discussing how he has wrestled with these issues when teaching about global sweatshops, Bigelow (2002) points out that he has "no desire to feign neutrality" because that only supports apathy and inaction (p. 132). Therefore, he tries to present both sides of issues as fairly as possible, while letting students know his own position. This tension between taking a stand and encouraging honest discussion does not always work itself out cleanly, but pushing students to look at more than one side of an issue prompts real thinking and honesty.

Helping Young People Learn to Prevent or Challenge Discrimination

Teachers cannot create caring classrooms by themselves; teaching children or youth to participate in caring means helping them to establish expectations to live by. Centralizing decision-making turns the teacher into the classroom "cop." This can undermine care in the classroom in at least two ways. First, centralizing decision-making does not help students learn to take ownership of rules for social living and of their own actions. It leaves them in a passive role. Second, children sometimes deliberately break rules set by the teacher as a way of challenging authority. If the teacher is the classroom cop, some children deliberately hurt other children to rebel against the cop figure.

An alternative to running a classroom like a dictatorship is to help students learn to exercise democratic decision-making within the classroom, involving them in making decisions about the work of the classroom. Sharing authority with students does not mean abdicating authority to them. Rather, it means guiding students in the process of learning to make decisions in a democratic fashion. A starting point is to help students brainstorm, discuss, and vote on rules and expectations for classroom behavior. Students can also help to establish consequences of behavior. Involving all students in this way helps them to develop ownership of caring behavior.

For example, students might decide that there will be no stealing. Many teachers encourage students to reword such an expectation, so that it tells students what they should do, rather than what they should not do, such as: "We will respect each other's property." What are the consequences of following this expectation or of failing to follow it? As students consider these kinds of questions, they can learn to act on caring and to take responsibility for their own behavior as well as the behavior of their peers.

These kinds of activities can help reduce prejudice and stereotyping. On the basis of a review of research on curricular interventions addressing racial and gender stereotyping (e.g., using a story where an Asian-American kid is having difficulty with mathematics and science to dispel the stereotype that all Asian kids are experts in these areas), J. A. Banks (1995) found that some studies report that interventions make no difference, whereas other studies report a positive change. Banks concludes that teachers should use curricular interventions and materials to help them, but they should pay attention to the impact of the interventions on students, so that they can make adjustments as needed. Young children seem particularly influenced by curricular interventions—elementary teachers have an especially important opportunity to develop open and democratic attitudes in children. [Later], we will again take up the issue of teaching for democratic participation.

Clubs that go beyond the walls of the classroom can also provide very helpful places for students to learn to work together to take stands on behalf of equity. For example, Gay-Straight Alliances (GSAs) have been in existence since 1988. GSAs, which generally meet during lunch or after school, "are open to all students and serve an especially important role for lesbian, gay, bisexual, and transgender (LGBT) students, children of LGBT parents, and straight student allies" (Macgillivary, 2007, p. 1). Macgillivary notes that research has found GSAs to reduce harassment as well as social isolation that LGBT students often experience.

Building Block 8: Using Cooperative Learning

Cooperative learning has a strong and consistent track record in improving student–student relationships across race, gender, and ability/disability lines as well as boosting student achievement (Bowen, 2000; E. Cohen & Lotan, 1997; Gillies & Ashman, 2000; D. W. Johnson, Johnson, & Maruyama, 1983; Slavin, Cheung, Groff, & Lake, 2008). Cooperative learning is a helpful strategy to embed within the larger philosophy of inclusive education. Loreman, McGhie-Richmond, Barber, and Lupart (2008) explain that, "Inclusive education involves schools and classrooms adapting the ways in which they work to ensure all students are educated together in common contexts, and are treated equitably." Inclusive education applies particularly to inclusion of students with disabilities across the full spectrum of schooling. Cooperative learning is especially useful in doing this because it makes constructive use of diverse learning abilities in the classroom.

Many teachers resist cooperative learning, confusing it with garden-variety group work. Reflection 3.11 asks you to reflect on your own experiences with group work. Write down (1) instances in which you remember group work being used when you have been a student; (2) what worked for you; and (3) what did not work for you.

Now let us compare group work you have experienced with four characteristics of cooperative learning: (1) heterogeneous grouping; (2) careful planning to make sure each student has a role; (3) work that requires interdependence of group members; and (4) students are taught cooperation and group process skills. In Reflection 3.12, these four characteristics appear in the left column. The right column asks you to compare instances of group work you described in Reflection 3.11 with these four characteristics.

How did the group work you have experienced fit those four characteristics? To what extent have you experienced cooperative learning?

> ### Reflection 3.11
>
> #### Group work
>
> When do you recall having participated in group work in school?
>
> What worked for you?
>
> What did not work for you?

> ### Reflection 3.12
>
> #### Characteristics of cooperative learning
>
> | Characteristics of cooperative learning | Group work you experienced |
> |---|---|
> | Groups are heterogeneous in terms of ability, race/ethnicity, gender, social class, etc. | |
> | Work is carefully planned, so that every student has a role; roles are switched as activities change; all students are accountable for their work. | |
> | Students must work together to complete the task; the task requires interdependence. | |
> | Students are taught cooperation, group process, and conflict resolution skills. | |

Let us look more closely at each of the four characteristics in relationship to building a caring classroom that supports achievement. Grouping students heterogeneously means mixing them by gender, racial or ethnic background, primary language, skill level, and so forth. Doing this disrupts patterns of segregation that may be developing among students and provides opportunities for them to get to know peers who differ from themselves. Heterogeneous grouping, when used along with the other three characteristics, makes diversity an asset to draw on rather than a problem to solve. For example, what kind of project might students be able to accomplish if one is a good writer, another is good at drawing, another is a good organizer, and yet another has strong computer skills? Of course, you would not want to pigeonhole students into using the same ability all the time rather than broadening their skills and abilities. But this example illustrates thinking of diversity as an asset to work with.

Cooperative learning requires planning, so that each student has a role. The biggest complaint usually lodged against group work is that a few students do most of the work whereas the others coast. Planning so each student has a role can take a variety of forms. For example, everyone in a group might have a different task to contribute to the group effort. Or, the group might be responsible for making sure all members learn material such as spelling words, because only one member will be called on to represent the group.

Students' roles must require interdependence—working and talking together. If students can complete a task through an assembly line process that does not require communication until the end when they assemble individually produced pieces, they will not reap the benefits of cooperative learning. The task must be structured, so they have to discuss, exchange ideas, or help each other.

Finally, the teacher needs to teach students how to cooperate. Most students do not automatically bring cooperation skills to class. Turn taking, encouraging others to speak, checking for understanding, or asking each other for help are behaviors that need to be learned. Teachers who can make cooperative learning work usually teach one or two cooperation skills at a time and start with fairly simple cooperative learning tasks. As students become better at engaging in cooperative learning, tasks can become more complex.

Student Dialogue 3.10

Celia: I enjoy working with other people, especially if there's enough guidance and structure so we know what we are doing. Without that, sometimes we just sit there and talk.

Gilbert: I don't enjoy it, or at least I haven't in the past because I end up doing most of the work. But if everyone had an assigned task, and we all knew what each person was responsible for, then maybe it wouldn't be so bad. I still might not like working in groups as well as I like working by myself, but at least it wouldn't be a real pain.

Lisa: I like the idea of having to interact about academics, as we are doing here. I'm learning quite a bit from the two of you. And I'm starting to learn to trust you.

Gilbert: Well, me too.

Various models of cooperative learning exist. The *group investigation model* requires students to contribute different talents, skills, interests, and roles to the creation of a group project or solving of a group problem. The project may be as elaborate as a multimedia production in which students synthesize information they have gathered about a topic, or it can be as small as a list of ideas generated during a short discussion (D. W. Johnson & R. T. Johnson, 1999). The *complex instruction model* organizes fairly open-ended problem-solving activities around a central concept or big idea. The activities are designed to require higher order thinking. Students are taught different roles that contribute to the task, such as "facilitator" and "materials manager." Teachers publicly identify something in particular that students are doing well and let the group know what is good about it, making sure that everyone gets recognized for doing something well, and that everyone is participating (E. Cohen & Lotan, 1997).

The *jigsaw model* involves two connected groupings. First, the class is divided into groups and each group studies a different but related subtopic of a larger topic. Group members work together to make sure they all understand the material and become "experts" on it. Students are then regrouped, so that each new group has one or two "experts" on each subtopic. A task is then given requiring students to pool their expertise. Many teachers like this model because it ensures that everyone has expertise to contribute. In the *team games model*, students practice academic skills while working together as a team. Then teams compete against other teams in a tournament. Team members have a vested interest in making sure everyone on the team has learned the material (Slavin, 1986).

It is fairly easy to find examples of cooperative learning, either by talking with teachers or on the Internet (although, oddly, given the strong research record of cooperative learning, many schools that are struggling to increase student achievement today are not using it because it is not part of tightly-scripted curriculum packages). Using whichever resource you have most access to, locate an example of each of the four models of cooperative learning for Reflection 3.13. Describe it briefly and then write a reflection on the strengths or weaknesses of that example.

Reflection 3.13

Examples of cooperative learning

Model	Example	Reflection
Group investigation		
Complex instruction		
Jigsaw		
Student team learning		

After you have completed Reflection 3.13, identify the example that seems least complicated, the one that you might be able to start with. As you work with reflective activities [...] that ask you to plan some curriculum and instruction, come back to Reflection 3.13 for examples of cooperative learning.

Putting It Into Practice
By Elizabeth Day and Kim Wieczorek (1998), University of Wisconsin–Madison

You are student teaching in Mrs. Stroman's third-grade classroom at Nolan Elementary School. The school is predominantly White and middle class, with a growing number of immigrant students. Some of them are from Mexico, and others are from Bosnia and Pakistan. In your student teaching classroom are two immigrant students—Carlos, who is new to the school and whose family is from Mexico, and Habiba, who came from Pakistan the previous year. So far as you can tell, things seemed relatively peaceful in the classroom—until last Friday.

Last Friday, Tracy, one of the White students, went home crying, telling her parents that Mrs. Stroman had grabbed her, spun her around, and in the process, hurt her. On hearing what happened, Tracy's father Bill Sloane called the principal who then set up a meeting for Monday morning.

At the meeting, Tracy hid her head in her mother's coat. Almost all the adults asked her to tell them what happened in the classroom. In a whisper, Tracy said that Mrs. Stroman had grabbed her and hurt her, because she took some paper away from some other classmates. But no one had asked her why she took the paper away. Mrs. Stroman explained that she had seen Tracy interrupting a small group of students who were working at a table near Tracy's seat. Tracy was talking loudly and had even started to grab a paper that one of the students was working on. Mrs. Stroman had gone over to Tracy and thought that Tracy had heard her say she should return to her own desk. When Tracy seemed to ignore her, Mrs. Stroman reached out her hand to physically guide Tracy back to her own seat. She certainly had not meant to hurt Tracy.

Mr. Tanner, the principal, lowered himself physically, so he was eye level with Tracy and asked her why she had grabbed the paper. Tearfully, Tracy said that it had some nasty words on it and a drawing of Habiba. Kids were making fun of Habiba, and Tracy did not know how to get them to stop, so she took their paper away. Then Mrs. Stroman had grabbed her and hurt her. Tracy was afraid and did not know what to do, because sometimes in the past she had made up stories in class, so people did not always believe her.

Mrs. Stroman looked bewildered for a moment and then asked Tracy if she still had the paper. Tracy said, no, it got torn up in the process, and she did not know where the pieces were. Mr. Tanner asked her how she knew that kids were making fun of Habiba.

Tracy replied, "They do it all the time on the playground. They know they'll get in trouble if a teacher hears, so they wait until a teacher isn't around."

As a student teacher, what would you do? What would you suggest that Mrs. Stroman do? Create a plan that addresses the immediate problems of this crisis, and a more long-term way of improving and building classroom relationships.

References

Aiello, B. (1979). Hey, what's it like to be handicapped? Practical ideas for regular class students and their teachers. *Education Unlimited*, 1(2), 28–31.

Alder, N. (2002). Interpretations of the meaning of care: Creating caring relationships in urban middle school classrooms. *Urban Education*, 37, 241–266.

Banks, J. A. (1995). Multicultural education: Its effects on students' racial and gender role attitudes. In J. A. Banks & C. M. Banks (Eds.), *Handbook of research on multicultural education* (pp. 617–627). New York: Macmillan.

Bell, L. I. (2002–2003, December/January). Strategies that close the gap. *Educational Leadership*, 60(4), 32–34.

Bigelow, B. (2002). The lives behind the labels. In B. Bigelow & B. Peterson (Eds.), *Rethinking globalization* (pp. 128–132). Milwaukee, WI: Rethinking Schools.

Bishop, R., Berryman, M., Cavanagh, T., & Teddy, L. (2009). Te Kotahitanga: Addressing educational disparities facing Maori students in New Zealand. *Teaching and Teacher Education*, 25, 734–742.

Bowen, C. W. (2000). A quantitative literature review of cooperative learning effects on high school and college chemistry achievement. *Journal of Chemical Education*, 77, 116–119.

Calabrese, R., Patterson, J., Liu, F., Goodvin, S., Hummel, C., & Nance, E. (2008). An appreciative inquiry into the Circle of Friends Program: The benefits of social inclusion of students with disabilities. *International Journal of Whole Schooling*, 4(2) 20–46.

Cirillo, K. J., Pruitt, B. E., Colwell, B., Kingery, P. M., Hurley, R. S., & Ballard, D. (1998). School violence: Prevalence and intervention strategies for at-risk adolescents. *Adolescence*, 33, 319–330.

Cohen, E., & Lotan, R. (Eds.). (1997). *Working for equity in heterogeneous classrooms*. New York: Teachers College Press.

D'Ambra, S. (2004). From conflict to a sustainable dialogue and peace. *International Journal of Curriculum and Instruction*, 6(1), 113–121.

Derman-Sparks, L. (1989). *Anti-bias curriculum: Tools for empowering young children*. Washington, DC: National Association for the Education of Young Children.

Drake, J. A., Price, J. H., & Telljohann, S. K. (2003). The nature and extent of bullying in school. *Journal of School Health*, 73, 173–180.

Eisler, R. (2000). *Tomorrow's children*. Boulder, CO: Westview.

Feshbach, N. D. (1975). Empathy in children: Some theoretical and empirical considerations. *Counseling Psychologist, 5*, 25–30.

Feshbach, N. D., & Feshbach, S. (1987). Affective processes and academic achievement. *Child Development, 58*, 1335–1347.

Finzi, R., Ram, A., Har-Even, D., Shnit, D., & Weizman, A. (2001). Attachment styles and aggression in physically abused and neglected children. *Journal of Youth and Adolescence, 30*, 769–786.

Fuller, M. L. (2001). Multicultural concerns and classroom management. In C. A. Grant & M. L. Gomez (Eds.), *Campus and classroom: Making school multicultural* (2nd ed., pp. 109–133). Upper Saddle River, NJ: Merrill Prentice-Hall.

Gallas, K. (1998). *Sometimes I can be anything*. New York: Teachers College Press.

Gathercoal, F. (1993). *Judicious discipline* (3rd ed.). San Francisco: Caddo Gap Press.

Gay, G. (2010). *Culturally responsive teaching: Theory, research, and practice* (2nd ed.). New York: Teachers College Press.

Gifford-Smith, M. E., & Brownell, C. A. (2003). Childhood peer relationships: Social acceptance, friendships, and peer networks. *Journal of School Psychology, 41*, 235–284.

Gillies, R. M., & Ashman, A. F. (2000). The effects of cooperative learning on students with learning difficulties in the lower elementary school. *Journal of Special Education, 34*(1), 19–27.

Girard, K., & Koch, S. (1996). *Conflict resolution in the schools: A manual for educators*. San Francisco: Jossey-Bass.

GLSEN Research Department. (2001). *The national school climate survey 2001: Lesbian, gay, bisexual, and transgender students and their experiences in schools*. New York: Gay, Lesbian and Straight Education Network.

Grant, C. A., & Sleeter, C. E. (2007). *Turning on learning* (4th ed.). New York: John Wiley.

Henning-Stout, M., James, S., & MacIntosh, S. (2000). Reducing harassment of lesbian, gay, bisexual, transgender, and questioning youth in schools. *School Psychology Review, 29*(2), 180–191.

Hoffman, D. M. (2009). Reflecting on social emotional learning: A critical perspective on trends in the United States. *Review of Educational Research, 79*, 533–556.

Institute for Education in Transformation. (1992). *Voices from the inside*. Claremont, CA: The Claremont Graduate School.

Irvine, J. J. (2003). *Educating for diversity: Seeing with a cultural eye*. New York: Teachers College Press.

Johnson, D. W., & Johnson, R. T. (1999). *Learning together and alone: Cooperative, competitive, and individualistic learning* (5th ed.). Boston: Allyn & Bacon.

Johnson, D. W., Johnson, R. T., & Maruyama, G. (1983). Interdependence and interpersonal attraction among heterogeneous and homogeneous individuals: A theoretical formulation and meta-analysis of the research. *Review of Educational Research, 53*, 51–54.

Juvonen, J. (2001). School violence: Prevalence, fears, and prevention. *Rand*. Retrieved August 16, 2005, from http://www.rand.org/publications/IP/IP219/

Kleinfeld, J. (1975). Effective teachers of Eskimo and Indian students. *School Review, 83,* 301–344.

Klem, A. M., & Connell, J. P. (2004). Relationships matter: Linking teacher support to student engagement and achievement. *Journal of School Health, 74,* 262–274.

Lemlech, J. K. (1991). *Classroom management: Methods and techniques for elementary and secondary teachers.* Waveland, IL: Waveland Press.

Lewis, A. E. (2003). *Race in the schoolyard.* New Brunswick, NJ: Rutgers University Press.

Loreman, T., McGhie-Richmond, D., Barber, J., & Lupart, J. (2008). Student perspectives on inclusive education: A survey of grade 3-6 children in rural Alberta, Canada. *International Journal of Whole Schooling, 5*(1), 1–15.

Macgillivary, I. K. (2007). *Gay-straight alliances: A handbook for students, educators, and parents.* Binghamton, NY: Hayworth Press.

Madhere, S. (1991). Self-esteem of African American adolescents: Theoretical and practical considerations. *Journal of Negro Education, 60*(1), 47–61.

Marx, S., & Pennington, J. (2003). Pedagogies of critical race theory: Experimentations with European-American pre-service teachers. *Qualitative Studies in Education, 16*(1), 91–110.

Meier, D. (2002). *In schools we trust.* Boston: Beacon Press.

Noddings, N. (1995). Teaching themes of care. *Phi Delta Kappan, 76*(9), 675–679.

Noddings, N. (2005). Caring in education. *The encyclopedia of informal education.* Retrieved August 9, 2005, from http://www.infed.org/biblio/noddings_caring_in_education.htm

Raider, E., & Coleman, S. (1992). *School change by agreement.* New York: Ellen Raider International.

Schultz, K. (2003). *Listening: A framework for teaching across differences.* New York: Teachers College Press.

Sears, J. T. (1993). Responding to the sexual diversity of faculty and students: Sexual praxis and the critically reflective administrator. In C. Capper (Ed.), *Educational administration in a pluralistic society* (pp. 110–172). Albany: SUNY Press.

Slapin, B., & Seale, D. (1998). *Through Indian eyes: The native experience in books for children.* Los Angeles: American Indian Studies Center, University of California.

Slavin, R. E. (1986). *Using student team learning.* Baltimore: The Johns Hopkins Team Learning Project.

Slavin, R. E., Cheung, A., Groff, C., & Lake, C. (2008). Effective reading programs for middle and high schools: A best evidence synthesis. *Reading Research Quarterly, 43,* 290–322.

Sleeter, C. E. (2001). *Culture, difference and power.* New York: Teachers College Press.

Sleeter, C. E. (2005). *Un-standardizing curriculum: Multicultural teaching in the standards-based classroom.* New York: Teachers College Press.

Steele, C. M., & Aronson, J. (1995). Stereotype threat and the intellectual test performance of African Americans. *Journal of Personality and Social Psychology, 69,* 797–811.

Sunburst Communication. (1994). *Student workshop: Conflict resolution skills*. New York: Houghton Mifflin.

Swearer, S. M., Espelage, D. L., Vaillancourt, T., & Hymal, S. (2010). What can be done about school bullying? *Educational Researcher, 39*(1), 38–47.

Tatum, B. D. (1997). *Why are all the black kids sitting together in the cafeteria?* New York: HarperCollins.

Thompson, A. (1998). Not the color purple: Black feminist lessons for educational caring. *Harvard Educational Review, 68*(4), 522–554.

U.S. Department of Education. (1998). *Status of educational equity for girls and women in the nation* (Vol. 2). Washington, DC: U.S. Government Printing Office.

Valentine, G. (1997). Ode to a geography teacher: Sexuality and the classroom. *Journal of Geography in Higher Education, 21*, 417–424.

Valenzuela, A. (1999). *Subtractive schooling: U.S.-Mexican youth and the politics of caring*. Albany: State University of New York Press.

Van Ausdale, D., & Feagin, J. R. (2001). *The first R: How children learn race and racism*. Lanham, MD: Rowman & Littlefield.

Zirkel, P. A. (2003). Bullying: A matter of law? *Phi Delta Kappan, 85*(1), 90–91.

Reading 4

What's Radical Love Got to Do with It

Navigating Identity, Pedagogy, and Positionality in Pre-Service Education

Ty-Ron M. O. Douglas and Christine Nganga

Critiques of teacher preparation and leadership programs have suggested that it is not enough to expose prospective teachers and school leaders to "best" practices of teaching linguistically, culturally, and ethnically diverse students. The need to develop the attitudes, knowledge, skills and dispositions necessary among pre-service educators for them to be competent to teach and lead a diverse student population has remained a major policy issue in U.S. teacher education (Horsford, Grosland, & Gunn; Milner, 2003; Zeichner & Liston, 1990). In a quest to continue the commitment to social justice and equity in public schools, there is still a lot that remains to be done pertaining to developing effective teachers who are culturally competent and critically conscious. The student population in U.S. schools continues to become increasingly different in background from the background of their teachers. Key researchers have broken ground in this area through their various perspectives on the issue of educating pre-service teachers and leaders—Gloria Ladson Billings (1995) on culturally relevant pedagogy, Geneva Gay (2000) on culturally responsive teaching, Brooks and Miles (2010) and Horsford, Grosland, and Gunn (2011) on culturally relevant leadership, Kenneth Zeichner (1983) on traditions of reform in teacher education and Christine Sleeter (2001) on preparing mainly white preservice teachers to teach diverse students. Their work has been influential in enhancing the knowledge of policy, theory, and practice in educating students effectively and highlighting what still needs to be done.

Ty-Ron Douglas and Christine Nganga, "What's Radical Love Got to Do With It: Navigating Identity, Pedagogy, and Positionality in Pre-Service Education," *The International Journal of Critical Pedagogy*, vol. 6, no. 1, pp. 58-82. Copyright © 2015 by The University of North Carolina at Greensboro. Reprinted with permission.

However Bartolomé (1994), Giroux (2005), and Wilson, Douglas, and Nganga (2013), among others, point out that the debate about improving minority academic achievement has often been reduced to a technical issue in policy texts and in preparation programs. Bartolomé (1994) further explains that the academic underachievement of minority students is often explained as a result of a lack of "cognitively, culturally, and/or linguistically appropriate teaching methods and educational programs" while "the solution to the problem of academic underachievement tends to be constructed in primarily methodological and mechanistic terms dislodged from the sociocultural reality that shapes it" (pp. 173–174). Further, the question of how teachers and leaders should be educated cannot be explored without taking into consideration the role of teacher education and leadership preparation programs in maintaining or transforming the institutional arrangements of schools and understanding the complex social, political, and economic patterns that are linked to schooling (Brunner, Hammel, & Miller, 2010; Sloan, 2009; Zeichner, 1983, 1993). In this regard, as scholars and educators of pre-service teachers and school leaders, we wish to extend this conversation using a critical pedagogical lens and specifically Paulo Freire's concept of *radical love* to interrogate our ways of teaching and opening up spaces for dialogue towards educating pre-service teachers and leaders who are critically conscious. Preparing to teach and lead a culturally and linguistically diverse student body warrants that educators examine their own values and assumptions about working with students who are different from them. Indeed, teacher educators such as Sleeter (2001) acknowledge that the cultural gap between students in the schools and the educators who teach and lead them continues to grow. Statistics confirm this cultural gap with the teaching work force being over 80% white (NCES, 2009). One's ideological posture informs and often times unconsciously colors the perceptions of teachers who work with diverse students (Bartolomé, 2004). Hence, it is important for pre-service teachers and those in leadership preparation programs from dominant cultures to have avenues in university classrooms where they can process issues pertaining to cultural differences, their uncertainties, and assumptions that they may have about the students they will teach and lead.

An important aspect of preparing teachers and leaders who are critically conscious is integrating and interrogating the positionalities of those who work with pre-service teachers and school leaders. In turn, the process of interrogating our positionalities as educators also allows us to incorporate pedagogies that offer pre-service teachers and school leaders an opportunity to interrogate who they are as future teachers of diverse student populations. In this paper, we therefore use Paulo Freire's concept of radical love to explore the similarities and disjunctures in our pedagogy and positionalities as international scholars of color. Specifically, we draw from our experiences teaching undergraduate and graduate pre-service teachers, and school leaders. The purpose of this [reading] is twofold—to discuss how our positionalities impact the practice of our teaching and to explore ways in which we enact radical love in our classrooms.

Defining *epistemology* and *positionality* is a necessary endeavor in this [reading], and so for the purposes of linguistic transparency and authorial catharsis, we acknowledge and accept that there are embedded complexities and challenges to amalgamating our voices, positionalities, and epistemologies into a coherent co-written manuscript. We persist with this highly nuanced project, rift with its own complexities, because of our commitments to social justice and anti-oppressive teaching. We embrace Dillard's (2003) admonition that "epistemology (how we know reality) is not a monolithic body, but is instead the ways in which reality is a deeply cultured knowing that arises from and embodies the habits, wisdom, and patterns of its contexts of origin" (p. 155). Said another way, one's epistemology is a highly nuanced filter that is constructed from an amalgamation of the social, political, and historical dynamics of lived experience. How we know reality is not a streamlined process that leads to a static end. Instead, much like one's positionality, the process of knowing shifts and morphs as variables and contexts change. In this light, we find Villaverde's (2008) definition of positionality to be powerful and apropos for this [reading] because it explicitly reveals the intersections between identities, epistemology, and positionality. Villaverde (2008) describes positionality as "how one is situated through the intersection of power and the politics of gender, race, class, sexuality, ethnicity, culture, language, and other social factors" (p. 10). Moreover, we seek to account for the complexity and diversity that inform our identities, our practices as educators in teacher-education classrooms, and our roles as researchers/scholar-practitioners who embrace elements of critical pedagogy and radical love in our praxis.

Pedagogy not oppression. There is a false assumption that pedagogy and teaching are necessarily synonymous. There are many teaching practices and ideologies that are not pedagogical in the Freirian sense, and these distinctions must be made explicit, through critical reflection, thoughtful interrogation, and conscientious inquiry if we are to honor the intent of Freire's (1970) manifesto, *Pedagogy of the Oppressed*, and more importantly, become critical agents of anti-oppressive education as a political project. Sadly, pre-service teachers and school leaders are given far too few opportunities to reflect on, inquire about, and interrogate who they are as human beings, developing pedagogues, and critical agents/facilitators of anti-oppressive 21st century classrooms and schools. This is not to suggest that there is a neat and unified approach to critical or anti-oppressive pedagogy. Our position is quite the opposite, in fact. Teachers who honor and embrace the Freirian tradition of pedagogy do not simply acknowledge and adjust to the messiness concomitant with critical reflection, thoughtful interrogation, and conscientious inquiry. Instead, these pedagogues are intentional about elucidating (and even creating) the inherent tensions, while respecting the "liminal spaces" (Villaverde, 2008) that members of the learning community will need to see the intersections between power, oppression, and pedagogy, *identify* their complicity in the status quo, and *embrace* their responsibility to act. Villaverde (2008) reminds us that "[t]here is no set way or process for pedagogy; it is ever evolving, organic, and dynamic" (p. 135). What is clear is that one's pedagogy (and leadership, for that matter) cannot be disassociated from power differentials and oppression, for and across individuals and institutions. Still, defining or describing *pedagogy* as the positionality of the teacher or leader in relation to these dynamics alone falls short of Freire's philosophy of education. Aronowitz (1993) declares that, the term he (Freire) employs to summarize his approach to education, 'pedagogy' is often interpreted as a 'teaching' method rather than a philosophy or a social theory. Few who invoke his name make the distinction. To be sure, neither does The Oxford English Dictionary. (p. 8) Macedo (2000) makes this distinction clear in describing pedagogy in his introduction to *30th Anniversary Edition of Pedagogy of the Oppressed*, where he points out that "education is inherently directive and must always be transformative" (p. 25). Macedo (2000) asserts that educators must understand that education is never neutral, even "as they engage in a social construction of not seeing" (pp. 24–25). For Villaverde (2008), "pedagogy sits at the intersection of understanding the systems of oppression, one's location within these, and one's agency in negotiating such experiences" (pp. 128–129). This broader conceptualization of pedagogy is vital to this analysis, because it lays the groundwork for understanding how revolutionary ideologies like critical pedagogy/ theory (of which Freire is often credited as the founder), engaged pedagogy (hooks, 1994), and even post-structural pedagogy are embodied in and operationalized within the context of *radical love* (as a pedagogical strategy/ approach). In the following section, we further explore critical pedagogy, radical love, and teacher identity in order to situate our own positionalities and praxis as teacher-educators who are committed to anti-oppressive, transformative pedagogy.

Critical Pedagogy

Critical pedagogy is an approach to education that involves liberation. Freire's work has been pertinent in furthering a critical pedagogical approach to education (Freire 1970, 1992, 2005). Other 20th century thinkers that have furthered this approach include McLaren (1999) and Bartlett (2005). Darder (1991) describes *critical pedagogy* as an

> educational approach rooted in the tradition of critical theory. Critical educators perceive their primary function as emancipatory and their primary purpose as commitment to creating the conditions for students to learn skills, knowledge, and modes of inquiry that will allow them to examine critically the role that society has played in their self-formation. (p. xvii)

In this respect, critical pedagogy is highly contextual and is neither a "recipe" nor a "method" (Darder, 1991). Villaverde (2008) offers this poignant description:

> Critical pedagogy aims to develop and nurture critical consciousness to address larger political struggles and transformations in dealing with rampant oppressive social conditions. It works from Paulo Freire's critique on the banking concept of education to chart new pedagogical experiences, carefully mining popular culture for a wide range of learning possibilities. A transformative pedagogy is made possible by the close investigation of margins and center (that is, of power) and through the cultivation of critical consciousness, praxis, and engagement of the self as a public change agent. (p. 129)

Further, Kincheloe (2008) asserts, "proponents of critical pedagogy understand that every dimension of schooling and every form of educational practice are politically contested spaces" (p. 2). The culture of schooling is not a neutral culture where every child naturally finds a sense of belonging. Teachers have to intentionally carry a disposition in their practice that enacts an inviting space for all students, including those who have been traditionally marginalized (Douglas & Peck, 2013).

Said differently, a critical pedagogical approach to education values learning experiences as an avenue for bringing forth social change by engaging in criticisms of capitalism, inequity, injustice, and other social ills that plague institutions and the larger society. Critique is never disassociated from the learners' responsibility to reflect on how they may be complicit in and beneficiaries of inequitable systems and disproportionate power relations. Critique is not an end in and of itself. It is only as effective as the learners' capacity to both question and ground their ideologies and those of the wider community within larger geo-political, socio-historical, and cultural constructs. Therefore, teachers who engage in critical pedagogical approaches are always informed about current issues pertaining to injustices and intentional about contextualizing and connecting these issues to the past. Critical pedagogy is a larger filter that undergirds conceptualizations of *radical love* which we discuss below.

Radical Love

Trying to establish a unified and universally accepted definition of love is an exercise in futility. And we will make no such attempt, since we respect that there are many interpretations of what love is and isn't based on various social, cultural, and spiritual traditions. Instead, for the sake of grounding our discussion of Freire's notion of *radical love* and our descriptions of how we mobilize his conceptualization in our own praxis, we believe it is necessary to acknowledge various understandings of *love*. *The New American Webster Handy College Dictionary* defines love as "affection for another person; an object of affection, a sweetheart; any strong liking or affection; (in games) a score of zero." Cunningham (2004) delineates between what she sees as "false love" and "real love" to suggest that: *real* love involves radical action. ... When we choose real love, we refuse to work within the system. We don't play by The Rules. In real love, we choose to speak not in the language of competition and violence, but in that of cooperation and compassion. The language of real love is simple and straightforward. It begins with self-acceptance. Once we begin to remove the superficial measures of beauty, success, and what's considered 'good and normal' from our lives, we start to move towards accepting people in all their flawed glory ... Real love can be as simple as a glass of water. (p. 37) Darder (2002) embraces a similar philosophy by asserting that love can be an anti-oppressive force used to resist exploitation.

Not surprisingly, there is disagreement among scholars on the various *types* of love as historically framed by Greek philosophers. While Helm (2005) asserts that there are three brands of *love* that are traditionally attributed to the Greek philosophical tradition, Lewis (1960) asserts that there are actually four types of love: *eros* ("romance"); *philia* (friendship); *storge* ("affection"); and *agape* ("unconditional love"). While Helm (2005) and Lewis (1960) disagree on the validity of *storge*, and the distinctions between the various brands of love are not always clear, there appears to be more consensus on the connections between *agape love* and spiritual traditions. For example, Ryoo, Crawford, Moreno, and McLaren (2009) "privilege" *agape love* as the most appropriate 'brand' for framing their conceptualization of *critical spiritual pedagogy*. Lewis (1960) contends that *agape love* is the brand of love that is described in 1 Corinthians 13, which is also described as the *love chapter*. Christian biblical tradition affirms that "love is patient, love is kind. It does not envy, it does not boast, it is not proud. It is not easily angered, it keeps no record of wrongs. Love does not delight in evil but rejoices in the truth. It always protects, always trusts, always hopes, always perseveres. Love never fails" (1 Corinthians 13: 4–8, NIV). 1 John 4: 18 suggests that "perfect love casteth out all fear." In this biblical text, there's the suggestion that the opposite of love is not hate but fear. While both hooks (2003) and Hanh (1993) suggest that fear is an impediment of love, hooks is intentional about highlighting the interconnectedness of spirituality, education, and love. Similarly, Hanh (1993) declares that "[t]he usual way to generate force is to create anger, desire, and fear. But these are dangerous sources of energy because they are blind, whereas the force of love springs from awareness, and does not destroy its own aims" (p. 84). These theoretical conceptualizations have interesting connections to Freire's understanding of *love*, and more specifically, *radical love*.

Freire's notion of love is not entirely dissimilar from the perspectives of many popular traditions. In fact, he asserts that "love is an act of courage, *not fear*. ... a commitment to others. ... [and] to the cause of liberation" (1970, p. 78). Equally significant is the centrality of dialogue to Freire's conceptualization of love, and by extension, the relevance of language and its inherent power. Freire (1993) declares:

> Dialogue cannot exist ... in the absence of a profound love for the world and for people. The naming of the world, which is an act of creation and re-creation, is not possible if it is not infused with love. Love is at the same time the foundation of dialogue and dialogue itself (p. 89).

It is on this foundation that Freire's conceptualization of *radical love* stands. For Freire, radical love requires a commitment to dialogue and the capacity to take risks for the benefit of those we teach and ourselves. One of the risks we must take as pedagogues is to relinquish oppressive practices in the classroom, such as *the banking system of education*, in which students are treated like empty receptacles. In place of trying to *fill* students with knowledge, *radical love* demands that we utilize dialogue as a means of subverting dominant positionalities, since [love] "cannot exist in a relation of domination" (Freire, 1993, p. 89). In this respect, Freire's conceptualization of dialogue is far more demanding than surface conversations: "Founding itself upon *love, humility,* and *faith,* dialogue becomes a horizontal relationship of which *mutual trust* between the dialoguers is the logical consequence" (Freire, 1993, p. 91, emphasis added). This is a high calling that seems diametrically opposed to traditional conceptions of schooling and common conceptualizations that many new and experienced teachers hold in the classroom. Freire's (1993) questioning in this regard is profound and worthy of extended consideration:

> How can I dialogue if I always project ignorance onto others and never perceive my own? How can I dialogue if I regard myself as a case apart from others—mere 'its' in whom I cannot recognize other 'I's'? How can I dialogue if I consider myself a member of the in-group of 'pure' men, the owners of truth and knowledge, for whom all non-members are 'these people' or the 'the great unwashed'? How can I dialogue if I start from the premise that naming the world is the task of an elite ... ? How can I dialogue if I am close to—and offended by—the contribution of others? How can I dialogue if I am afraid of being displaced, the mere possibility causing me torment and weakness? Self-sufficiency is incompatible with dialogue. ... At the point of encounter there are neither utter ignoramuses nor perfect sages; there are only people who are attempting, together, to learn more than they now know. (p. 90)

In many respects, Freire's questioning above is the antithesis of traditional conceptualizations of what it means to teach. For one thing, far too few pre-service educators were/are challenged to reflect on these questions prior to entering the sacred space of the classroom. Without doubt, Freire (1970) would assert that this reality exists for the same reason that problem-posing education is unpopular in many schools: "[it] does not and cannot serve the interests of the oppressor. No oppressive order could permit the oppressed to begin to question: Why?" (p. 86). Notably, undergirding dialogue is an active *hope* and a commitment to *critical thinking* that is never disassociated from fearless action—all of which are always more potent than "false love, false humility, and feeble faith" (pp. 91–92). For those who claim or seek to educate, Freire's emphasis on communication, critical thinking, and dialogue as hallmarks of true education demand that radical love is extricated from the realm of the ephemeral so that our daily, horizontal interactions with humanity—in our classrooms and beyond—become the barometer by which we judge our praxis.

A profound love for humanity, coupled with a love for our subject matter and the power of ideas, must be present in order to teach—since teaching requires a love for the people and a love for the world (Darder, 2002; Freire, 1993, 1998). In fact, Freire staunchly believed that "teaching is an act of love" (Darder, 2002). McLaren (2000) described this love as "the oxygen of revolution, nourishing the blood ... [and] spirit of struggle" (as cited in Darder, 2002, p. 148). As teachers of future educators and proponents of *radical love*, we recognize that we must equip our students with tools that they can use to liberate themselves from forms of ignorance and oppressive practices in order to embrace and enact "a revolutionary pedagogy" (Darder, 2002, p. 148) in their own classrooms. Radical love, as a theorization that privileges the voices and perspectives of marginalized voices and non-dominant positionalities/perspectives, allows us to recast power differences in our classrooms, even as it provides tools for dialogue, action, and hope.

Teacher Identity

In exploring our teaching through the concept of *radical love* we offer a space where educators have a better understanding of the "self" they bring to the classroom in addition to the historic, social, cultural and political forces that have played a role in how they perceive themselves as future teachers and leaders. Scholars who explore *teacher identity* have mainly explored the concept within the framework of professional and personal aspects of teaching, such as effectiveness and commitment in teaching, subject matter expertise, student relationships and collegial relationships, dispositions, values and beliefs towards teaching (Day, 2002; Day & Kington, 2008; Walkington, 2005). Additionally, even for those who explore teacher identity among pre-service teachers, such as Danielewicz (2001) and Olsen (2009) who utilize a holistic view of how teacher education programs impact the teacher-self that is emerging, their work—though significant—does not focus on the social, historical and political factors that shape the ideological stances of teachers. Specifically, how those ideologies are linked to issues of power and privilege is not made explicit. We wish to incorporate the sociopolitical factors that impact teacher identity and thus the perspectives they bring to the classroom about teaching and leading diverse learners. We acknowledge that identity markers such as race, ethnicity, class or gender are not static but fluid. In this regard, Cochran-Smith (1995) contends that it is crucial for educators to understand their identity with this kind of examination, beginning with investigating our own histories as educators—"our own cultural, racial, and linguistic backgrounds and our own experiences as raced, classed, and gendered children, parents, and teachers in the world" (p. 500). For this reason, there is need for educators in teacher education and leadership programs to incorporate the socio-cultural and political dimensions of identity to the professional and personal aspects to helping pre-service teachers and leaders understand who they are and how the self impacts their practice.

The works of Florio-Ruane with de Tar (2001) and Cooper (2007) are particularly useful in linking the personal-professional dimensions of teacher identity with the socio-cultural and political dimensions in helping pre-service teachers understand how who they are impacts how they teach. Florio-Ruane focuses on the dialectical relationship between the teacher and the diverse student body that preservice teachers will teach by using autobiographies of authors of diverse backgrounds, with the aim that "in their conversational responses to those writers and texts, teachers can awaken to their own experiences of their culture, especially those that influence their work as educators" (Florio-Ruane & de Tar, 2001, p. xxvi–xxvii). In his review of Florio-Ruane's text, Sloan (2004) adds that "while reading such texts by teachers is a way for them to learn about lived experiences of persons whose backgrounds are different from their own, the real power of such texts lies in their potential to foster reflexivity about teachers' own cultural identities" (p. 119). Indeed, Florio-Ruane and de Tar point out that conversations of such texts need to go beyond comfortable narratives of self and society in order to unsettle conventional notions of culture. Embracing an identity that entails teaching for diversity then requires the act of interrogating other people's experiences against the backdrop of one's own.

While Florio-Ruane and de Tar (2001) privilege cultural texts as the avenue through which identity work happens among pre-service teachers, Cooper (2007) places significance on community-based learning as an avenue for pre-service teachers to locate their professional selves by correcting misconceptions about culturally and linguistically diverse students. Through incorporating a series of activities in her course such as writing one's own autobiography and "walking a mile in another's shoes," Cooper noticed a shift in pre-service teachers' views and beliefs about the students they teach, as well as their families and the communities in which they live begin. The "connected sequential activities" they embark on allows them to learn "(a) who they are, (b) who they want to appear to be, and (c) who they are but do not want others to see" (Cooper, 2007, p. 253). In so doing, pre-service teachers critically examine their ideologies about teaching diverse learners. Thus, developing a professional identity is not just a matter of examining "who am I as a teacher, but additionally "who am I as a teacher of diverse learners?" This is an important component of identity work among pre-service teachers that has heavily influenced how we think about our teaching and scholarship.

Interrogating Our Positionalities and Epistemologies

In order to evaluate how we navigate our identities, pedagogies, and positionalities (as well as those of our students) in our work as educators, it is necessary to make the connections between these concepts explicit. We see our positionalities and pedagogy as two interrelated concepts that are grounded in and outgrowths of various elements of personal, cultural, and community identity. Despite the many scholars who have commented on the social constructedness of the concepts of race, class, and gender (Dillard, 2003; Douglas, 2012; Fine, Weis, Weseen, & Wong, 2000; Gresson, 2008; hooks, 2000; Johnson, 2006; Omi & Winant, 1986; Schwalbe, 2005), there appears to be a reluctance in scholarly discourse to consistently interrogate the impact of socially constructed knowledge and "patterns of epistemology" (Dillard, 2003). As a result of this reluctance, many people also fail to see the social constructedness and constructive (or destructive, depending on one's positionality) powers of research (Dillard, 2003) and pedagogy. In this respect, post-formal thinking is significant in expanding the narrow conceptualizations of intelligence in order to uncover how particular communities (usually non-white, poor, and feminine) have been excluded and marginalized (Kincheloe & Steinberg, 1993). Much like critical pedagogy, "post-formal thinking works to get behind the curtain of ostensible normality," and post-formal thinkers/ teachers "work to create situations that bring hidden assumptions to our attention and make the tacit visible" (Kincheloe & Steinberg, 1993, p. 306). For example, critical pedagogues/post-formal thinkers challenge how research has been used historically to *scientifically prove* the inferiority of minority groups (Dodson, 2007; Kincheloe & Steinberg, 1993; Kincheloe, Steinberg, & Gresson III, 1996). Critical pedagogues not only acknowledge how teachers have used their positionalities and classroom powers to reinforce oppressive paradigms in the minds, hearts, and report cards of students; additionally, through their praxis, they work against systems of domination for the good of all students.

Research and pedagogy are shaped by people, social contexts, and institutional forces, even as they also shape people (and perceptions of people), social contexts, and institutional forces. Ladson-Billings (2000) hints at the multiple ways in which knowledge construction and research intersect by reminding us that "epistemology is more than a 'way of knowing.' An epistemology is a 'system of knowing' that has both an internal logic and external validity" (p. 257). Moreover, as pedagogues and researchers, we inform others (and ourselves), as we stand on and speak from the (mis)understandings and (mis)interpretations of our own positionalities, our own identities, and our research. In the subsequent sections, we seek to account for the complexity and diversity of identity and positionality in our own experiences as scholar-practitioners, recognizing that there are distinct similarities and differences in who we are and how we teach.

Learning to Teach and Teaching to Learn: Christine's Reflection

Naming who I am as an educator and scholar is problematic. One of the reasons is because I believe that identity (whether as an educator or as a person) is fluid, multiple and dependent upon social, political, historical and cultural forces. I have been acted upon as I act upon these forces in the multiple worlds that I have lived and continue to live in. I do believe as Taylor, Tisdell and Hanley (2000) affirm that my positionality and that of the students impact the classroom dynamics and how we construct knowledge in this shared space. Though I may be perceived to have some level of power as the instructor, I am also aware that my ethnicity (coming from a different country of origin) warrants questioning regarding my capacity to understand and analyze issues of diversity and difference in foreign soil, in this case a U.S. university classroom. I also realize that how I am positioned by my students may be different from how I position myself. My ways of knowing what I know and how I utilize that knowledge is culturally nuanced by my background that has been impacted by having studied in an educational system that still bears the markers of Britain as Kenya is a former colony. I am also aware that I may be (and often have been) viewed by students and professionals in the academy as a "native informant" who knows everything about Africa and may speak for Africans in an academic space. I therefore wrestle with my teaching within and between the intersections of who I think I am and who I am perceived to be. In this regard, Freire's concept of radical love offers me a footstool on which to stand as I enact my teaching. I accept his call to take risks in the classroom, and embrace the courage to teach (Palmer, 1998) while creating spaces of dialogue (even uncomfortable conversations).

In seeking to teach as an act of love, I conceptualize that kind of love as one that critically challenges the way we think and act by denying being a part of a dehumanizing education even when the system constantly beckons educators to be such, but instead embrace a liberatory educational practice as Freire admonishes. Indeed, love is the basis of education that seeks justice and equality for all (Kincheloe, 2008).

I embrace a love for humanity, for the students I teach, for self, and for others. I cannot have the courage to teach if I do not care enough for my students and the larger humanity whom they will impact. I understand that this is not an easy task. I must guard myself against the inflictions of fear and intimidation as an upcoming scholar-practitioner who seeks not only to unsettle issues of power and privilege within U.S. schools but to help my students understand the global world that we live in—that one nation's decisions impacts other nations as well. I therefore stretch the dismantling of issues of power and privilege in my classroom not only to reach U.S. classrooms but also to sensitize students to an awareness that we live in an interconnected world and to examine how the U.S. utilizes its international space to consider how issues such as economic trends, social ills, impacts other nations including developing nations.

I am a firm believer in co-constructing knowledge in the classroom. However, I am also aware that the ways of knowing and what we know that we bring into the classroom are sometimes problematic, especially when layered with oppressive notions, deficit thinking, and "I am better than you" attitudes. Therefore, for me embracing a pedagogy of radical love also includes helping students to analyze the roots of their knowledge basis and often times offering tools to garden different roots for what they come to believe and know about themselves, society, and the students they will teach. Hence a humanizing education must embrace a "deeply reflective interpretation of the dialectical relationship between our cultural existence as individuals and our political and economic existence as social beings" (Darder, 2009, p. 568). I am committed to this way of educating, knowing and being.

Enacting Radical Love in the Classroom

Over the course of my doctoral work, I taught a course called *Diverse Learners* to pre-service and alternative licensure teachers and a similar course as faculty to school leaders in preparation. This course was designed to provide students with a broad base of knowledge and skills that will facilitate their effectiveness in meeting the needs of diverse learners through appropriate instructional, curricular, and behavioral strategies. Students also explored diversity with respect to race, ethnicity, socioeconomic class, language, gender and exceptionalities. The majority of the students were white and came from varying socioeconomic backgrounds. I was cognizant of the complexities of teaching in a university classroom where none of the voices are silenced even when those voices are not of the majority. I concur with Montecinos (2004) who points out that instructors in teacher education programs should not simply be concerned about training white teachers to teach diverse learners. Pre-service students of color can also benefit from such courses by validating the cultural knowledge they bring and helping them translate it into a libratory pedagogy. Additionally, students from poor and working class backgrounds need to affirm their own agency even as they sometimes "express frustration, anger and sadness about the tensions they experience in trying to conform to acceptable white middle class behaviors in university settings" (hooks, 1994, p. 182). Teaching in a classroom within such complexities is not an easy venture. However, even within such complexities and tensions, I found three interrelated aspects of enacting a pedagogy of radical love that helps me to remain true to what I believe about teaching and learning and to offer pre-service teachers a classroom space where they could have the freedom and the safety to examine who they were as well as the knowledge they bring about teaching culturally, ethnically and linguistically different populations. These were building community, creating dialogic spaces, and critical reflective practice.

Building community. Building community among students is a beginning point in creating a space for enacting radical love in the classroom. Palmer (1998) with whom I concur, believes that teaching, learning, and knowing happens through a communal web of relationships. Creating a sense of community in the classroom helps the instructor to step away from the banking method of education that Freire strongly reproves of. In teaching within a community, students are regarded as a "reservoir of knowledge" and the teacher's role varies from "facilitator to co-learner" (Palmer, 1998, p. 116). Indeed, Freire believes that students and teachers simultaneously carry both embodiments. Building community helps every student to feel valued and like their experiences matter even when they are different from the majority. Second, it is also a forum to understand that the realities of lived experiences are varied both for the pre-service teachers and for the future students they will teach. It is within community that students and teachers can have authentic dialogue and that education becomes a process of inquiry in which students and the instructors are all engaged in the process of co-constructing knowledge.

Creating Dialogic Spaces. Teacher education classrooms need to be spaces where students can question

> the omissions and tensions that exist between the master narratives and the hegemonic discourses that make up the official curriculum and the self representations of subordinated groups as they might appear in 'forgotten' or erased histories, histories, texts, memories, experiences and community narratives. (Giroux, 2005, p. 25)

Such spaces can either be in traditional classroom spaces, through electronic media, and in large or small groups. Offering students multiple spaces for dialogue has proved to be functional and constructive. For students who are less forthcoming in larger settings, they seem to find their voice in smaller groups. Additionally, online discussion groups provide forums where students can dialogue about the course material using directed prompts when they do not meet in traditional classrooms. Second, when students respond to one another through online discussions, they are able to see how their assumptions continue to be challenged from the beginning of the course to the end. Respect for all is required in these discussions. This kind of dialogue "requires an intense faith in human kind to make and remake, to create and re-create, faith in their vocation to be more fully human (Freire, 1970, p. 90).

Critical Reflective Practice. Critical reflection among pre-service educators is crucial in helping them uncover biases, assumptions and beliefs about teaching students who are culturally, ethnically and linguistically different (Howard, 2003; Miller, 2003). As an avenue to uncover their biases, beliefs and assumptions about each aspect of diversity, students respond to prompts taken from the course readings and materials. In this regard, it is important to expose pre-service educators to course materials that offer them the opportunity to understand aspects of systemic inequalities in schools and societies as well as what they can do as teachers and leaders in their classrooms, schools, and communities. Critical reflective practice in this way helps them to situate their beliefs with the current literature on aspects of diversity and to subsequently build on their own future practice in teaching and leadership.

Building community, creating dialogic spaces, and critical reflective practice cannot be treated as isolated elements of enacting the concept of radical love. Each of them enhances the others. When students feel a sense of belonging in a learning community, their uncertainties do not become barriers to learning as they discover how to challenge reductionistic notions of schooling and education.

Pedagogue as Border Crosser: Ty's Reflection on Positionality

As a Christian, Black (African Bermudian/American), heterosexual man, I recognize that it is a privilege and responsibility to be in the academy at this time. I believe that my unique background affords me the opportunity to transcend cultural borders as an educator, researcher and scholar. Still, I recognize that I can be viewed with some degree of suspicion and distrust by those who hold different views, particularly if these views have been influenced by distasteful experiences with institutions and individuals who utilize similar labels to the ones that reflect elements of my positionality. For instance, as a Christian, I recognize that more people have been killed in the name of God than any other name; as a Black man, I also understand that despite the accomplishments of inspirational Black men like President Obama and Dr. King, Black men are still, by in large, expected to emulate the characteristics espoused by the media—criminals, athletes, and dead-beats (Gause, 2008). The image of men as egotistical, unfaithful brutes, in addition to the changing roles of men, both influence my role as an educator and researcher because they influence how I know reality; moreover, my epistemology has been shaped by socio-cultural practices and norms in Bermuda and the United States that espouse particular brands of Black masculinity. As a Black Bermudian/American male who has been afforded the opportunity to prepare educators in the United States, I am both an insider and an outsider on multiple levels—a border crosser. Still, my positionality encompasses more than my ethnic background and national affiliations.

Naming how my beliefs as a Seventh-day Adventist Christian inform and intersect with my work as a scholar-practitioner is a necessary step if I am to honestly account for my subjectivity in the classroom and define my positionality. By drawing on what some would describe as primitive Biblical principles, in one sense my positionality as a Seventh-day Adventist reflects traditional Christianity; yet, in another sense, it is far from traditional in that it espouses teachings that are no longer common in traditional or mainstream Christianity. For example, unlike many who reduce Christianity to a religion of New Testament teachings, my perspective encompasses the whole Bible as the standard for truth, hope, and wisdom in ways that many nominal Christians no longer acknowledge or accept—this includes adherence to all of the Ten Commandments. Drawing from the work of Peshkin (1988), I have determined that all of my "I"s are undergirded by my primary researcher positionality as a *non-traditional Christian intellectual*. I have determined that my other (more specific) "I"s include, but are not limited to: the non-traditional Christian Intellectual/ Witness I; the Husband and Father I; the Family/People Centered I; the Black Masculinity I; the African Bermudian/ American I; the Ethnic and International Difference I; the Border Crossing I; the Questioning of the Establishment/Authority/Status Quo I; the Respectfully Rebellious I; and the Critically Hopeful I. All of these lenses intersect to impact my gaze and role as an educator, researcher and scholar.

Wrestling with radical love. I continue to wrestle with Freire's notion of *radical love*. I question whether the term radical love is even appropriate to use to describe our daily human interactions. My discomfort is rooted in the belief that *love* is one of the most abused concepts in the human experience. I believe the capacity to love, radically or otherwise, is a gift from God. More than that, I believe that God is love (1 John 4: 8). In fact, my initial thoughts upon hearing the term *radical love* used in an academic setting raced to reflections of Christ hanging on a cross for the sake of humans who would reject Him. In this context, Freire's notion is not radical or loving enough, I thought. Certainly, Freire wasn't asking me to give my life for someone else ... or was he? My questioning of whether the term radical love was/is an appropriate describer for our daily human interactions is rooted in my belief that much of what we do as humans is actually rooted in selfishness and fear, rather than love. In spite of my initial discomfort, I began to conceptualize what *radical love* could look like in the classroom. Recognizing and respecting that individuals embrace various spiritual and existential positions,

I wondered how this notion of *radical love* could be reeled in from its perch and operationalized so that it is not reduced to lofty, overstated language.

As I reflected on what I see as radical love personified—Christ's sacrifice for humanity, I was reminded that He did not simply offer Himself as *the* sacrifice; in addition, He lived a life *of* sacrifice. His life was not merely about moments. His life was devoted to ministry. Biblical record suggests that Jesus engaged in a (radical) pedagogy that challenged the religious leaders of His day and is a far cry from nominal Christianity today, where the tangible needs and pain of human beings seem to be obscured by mere church attendance, emblems on a chain, and sermonic overtures. In this context, dialogue has been replaced with dogmatism, passion for the destitute has been usurped by prejudice, and love has been kidnapped by lip-service on one extreme and legalism on the other. Sadly, some of the most damaging and divisive language runs off the lips of people who would self-identify as Christians. This pattern is typified by the disturbing billboard posted by a *Christian* minister in Kansas after the election of Barak Obama: "America, we have a Muslim president. This is a sin against the Lord." Certainly, the abuse of God and religion has caused many to echo the words of Mahatma Ghandi: "I like your Christ, I do not like your Christians. Your Christians are so unlike your Christ." In this light, I realized that the challenge to operationalize *radical love* is a personal one: I reflected on my praxis. Pedagogically speaking, I thought about what sacrificing my life for my students looks like. Ultimately, I sought a balanced interpretation of *radical love* as a pedagogical imperative for all educators, understanding and respecting that there are a variety of life philosophies, spiritual traditions, existential allegiances, and belief systems that inform how we think, feel, act, and teach: some choose to eschew any notion of faith; others aim to live a life of faith; and still others operate on a continuum somewhere in-between. For Freire (1970), faith in humanity (along with an abiding trust and hope) is critical to our capacity for dialogue.

Radical Love, Radical Pedagogy

Teaching a course for undergraduate pre-service teachers on the "institution of education" and similar graduate courses for school leaders has allowed me to enact *radical love*, engage in radical pedagogy, and reflect on my positionality and responsibility as an educator. As I engaged in these processes, I was encouraged by the work of scholars like Freire (1970), Dillard (2000), West (1982, 1993), Dantley (2005), and hooks (1994), who (in their own ways) name how spirituality undergirds who they are and the risks they take for the sake of the educational advancement of their students. Even now, as an emerging scholar who sees spirituality as central to my work in the academy, I can relate to the "spiritual crisis" and tensions Cozart (2010) experienced as a result of her "belief that spirituality was a separate layer of marginalization, separate from race and gender ... [which caused her to act] as if spirituality was a third consciousness, rather than part of my merging double-consciousness into a better truer self" (p. 253). Like Cozart, I have no desire to live, teach or lead from such an oppressive paradigm, even as I embrace the inherent risks that emerge anytime one names her/his positionality. I understand and embrace these risks, knowing that, at times, it feels easier and safer to discuss issues of race, class, gender, and sexuality in the academy than it does to dialogue about issues of spirituality. Clearly, there are a number of reasons that can account for this reality, including the tendency and tensions created by the conflation of spirituality with religion and religious experiences (Cozart, 2010; Dantley, 2005; Douglas & Peck, 2013), respect for separation of church and state legislation, and the personal nature of spirituality. Frankly, to encourage dialogue and investigation around issues of spirituality is risqué—radical even. To be clear, I feel the tension now as I attempt to articulate some of the strategies I utilize in my classroom. Still, I draw strength from my commitment to my students and my praxis, understanding that, there is an aspect of our vocation that is sacred

> ... our work is not merely to share information but to share in the intellectual and spiritual growth of our students. To teach in a manner that respects and cares for the souls of our students is essential if we are to provide the necessary conditions where learning can most deeply and intimately begin. (hooks, 1994, p. 13)

More than that, I teach, lead, and live by the mantra that "perfect love casteth out all fear" (1 John 4: 18) or in the words of Freire (1970), "love is an act of courage, not fear. ... a commitment to others. ... [and] to the cause of liberation" (p. 78).

Going beyond 'middle people.' Many of my students have expressed their discomfort and fear of discussing topics like religion/spirituality in their other course experiences. Colleagues who embrace various religious/ spiritual traditions have expressed similar sentiments to me. Having taught in somewhat conservative communities, including areas in the Bible-belt, I understand that many of my students enter my classroom with prior knowledge and experiences with some form of religion. Ironically, this topic is rarely broached within the context of their identities as educators and individuals who wrestle with their beliefs.

In my classroom, I emphasize the importance of dialogue, recognizing that it is a means through which transformation can begin, relationships are developed, and mutual respect is forged. I also emphasize the importance of reading and researching primary documents for ourselves. For example, we discuss how religion—particularly Christianity in the U.S.—has been abused and used as a means of oppression and domination. My students are usually astounded by what they learn about Christopher Columbus and his disturbing exploits in the name of God (Loewen, 2007). As students try to reconcile the purpose for and means by which they will teach their students about Columbus (in light of their new knowledge), they are also challenged with the reality that most school textbooks herald Christopher Columbus as a brilliant hero. These revelations and discussions often propel students to declare: "what else haven't we been told and why have these truths been kept from us?" Through various exercises and activities, I challenge students to research and consider contemporary manifestations of these dynamics, particularly as it relates to textbooks. In this context, spiritual/biblical texts are textbooks. Students are encouraged to bypass the "middle people" (my gender-sensitive adaption of "the middle men")—i.e. teachers, pastors, rabbis, bishops, priests—in order to engage in their own study of primary and secondary documents. Students are encouraged to dialogue with the documents in whatever manner they deem appropriate: listening, responding, contesting, interrogating, meditating, and praying are options that some students utilize to dialogue with the documents. I give no parameters for how students should engage in this research, except that they look at the documents for themselves and allow their previously held perspectives to be challenged. For me, this is not a sneaky evangelistic strategy. This is about encouraging future teachers to develop the agency to challenge paradigms and institutions, understanding that the schoolhouse is not the only *institution of education* (Douglas, in press; Douglas & Peck, 2013; Khalifa, Dunbar, & Douglas, 2013).

Students often research common assumptions that are grounded in historical, political, and religious traditions: for example, students are often amazed when they uncover that the history of Sunday observance as the Sabbath is rooted in the dictates of Emperor Constantine and the Roman Catholic Church, rather than the Bible. Other students challenge the history and validity of the Bible, and discussions about whether there are actually lost books of the Bible or who actually wrote the Bible become platforms for deeper dialogue and inquiry into power, language, positionality, and institutions (of education). We also reflect on how racism is institutionally perpetuated in religious settings today; for example, we challenge what Black church/White church dichotomies reveal about humanity and the Christian church. We question children's literature that portrays angels as exclusively White and male. We look at gender roles—in particular, the oppression of women in some biblical cartoon portrayals. We also interrogate the assumption that America is a Christian nation. These activities push students to reflect on their individual and collective identities, their positionalities, and the implications these dynamics have for their praxis.

Fear factor. When students first walk into my classroom, I sense that they bring with them many fears. Some are afraid to fail; some are afraid to talk; some are afraid to sound obtuse, while others seem to be afraid of each other ... or at least afraid to talk to each other; then there are those who appear to be afraid of me, in the sense that I am the one who supposedly holds the power. As an instructor who hasn't forgotten what it feels like to be a student, I have come to know many of these fears all too well. As I help my students unpack these dynamics throughout the semester, it also becomes clear that most of these pre-service teachers and leaders are also afraid of not being in *control* of their students or the learning process. For many of these future teachers and leaders, to be publically challenged by a student or to not know the *correct answer* to a student's question is an unpardonable sin. For me, *radical love* demands that I challenge these fears and help them to relinquish the belief that they can actually control the learning process or the learning spaces that function beyond the walls of their classrooms.

Learning from community-based pedagogical spaces. Teachers, administrators, and policy makers continue to ignore the impact of non-school based educative locales on students. Community-based pedagogical spaces are "non-school based locales, institutions, forces, or methods that have been/ are utilized for educational purposes," such as the media, music, churches, barbershops, hair salons, sports clubs/fields, and theaters (Douglas, in press; Douglas & Gause, 2009; Douglas & Peck, 2013). Drawing on the tradition of historical scholarship and the works of Freire (1970) and Cremin (1970, 1980, 1988), scholars who embrace the breadth of what it means to educate, I utilize a community-based pedagogical space assignment to encourage students to talk to people and learn from spaces outside of traditional classrooms. Pre-service teachers and leaders are challenged to consider where and how learning takes place. Much like educators fear losing control in their classrooms or not knowing a correct answer, there also seems to be a fear of acknowledging or embracing the educative power of spaces outside of the schoolhouse. As an act of radical love, this is a fear that I try to dismantle and challenge in my work with pre-service teachers.

As I challenge my students to face the fear and contradictions of lived experiences inside and outside of the classroom, I simultaneously challenge them to reflect on the risks that will be necessary if they are to share a sense of hope through their pedagogy and leadership. The outcomes of these processes are not always fully apparent to me. I often remind my students that *the process is more important than the product; in fact, the process is the product*. Often, the fruits of the process are readily apparent in students who exit the course more committed to a social justice agenda. Ultimately though, this process-based approach is rooted in the hope and faith that I have in my students to continue the inquiry process that is promoted in my class. Where the journey leads them is beyond my influence and jurisdiction. My responsibility is to give them tools and opportunities to challenge oppressive systems and ideals. It's a process that I continue to engage in personally. Even as I participate in and name particular positionalities, systems and ideologies, my position as a non-traditional Christian intellectual is not a passive one: I am willing to name and challenge "injustice anywhere," recognizing that it is always "a threat to justice everywhere" (King, 1963, p. 1854).

Conclusion: Radical Love as Process and Product

Enacting radical love in our classrooms has become a way to take risks in having conversations about the socio-cultural dynamics imbedded in our positionalities, our identities as instructors, and the positionalities and identities of our students. It is an approach in our teaching that helps us to stay true to the ideals of critical pedagogical approaches, while still modeling a more humanizing way of teaching and learning for our students. As leaders of pre-service teachers, we believe that: *having a position* is expected; *knowing* your position is important; *naming* one's positions is vital, but *critically reflecting* on how your *havings*, *knowings*, and *namings* may impact your interactions with students is the difference between preparing to teach/lead and preparing to be an anti-oppressive pedagogue and leader who will radically love all students.

References

Aronowitz, S. (1992). *The politics of identity: Class, culture and social movements*. New York: Routledge.

Bartolomé, L. (1994). Beyond the methods fetish: Toward a humanizing pedagogy, *Harvard Educational Review*, 64(2), 173–194.

Bartolomé, L. (2004). Critical pedagogy and teacher education: Radicalizing prospective teachers. Teacher Education Quarterly, 31(1), 97–122.

Brooks, J. S., & Miles, M. T. (2010). Educational leadership and the shaping of school culture: Classic concepts and cutting-edge possibilities. In S. Douglass Horsford (Ed.), *New possibilities in educational leadership: Exploring social, political, and community contexts and meaning* (pp. 7–28). New York: Peter Lang.

Brunner, C. C, Hammel, K, & Miller, M. D. (2010). Transforming leadership preparation for social justice: Dissatisfaction, inspiration, and rebirth—an exemplar. In S. Douglass Horsford (Ed.), *New possibilities in educational leadership: Exploring social, political, and community contexts and meaning* (pp. 261–277). New York: Peter Lang.

Cochran-Smith, M. (1995). Color blindness and basket making are not the answers: Confronting the dilemmas of race, culture, and language diversity in teacher education. *American Educational Research Journal*, 32(3), 493–522.

Cooper, J. (2007). Strengthening the case of community-based learning in teacher education. *Journal of Teacher Education*, 58(3), 245–255.

Cozart, S. C. (2010). When the spirit shows up: An autoethnography of spiritual reconciliation with the academy. *Educational Studies*, 46(2), 250–269.

Cunningham, V. (2004). Radical love. *Off Our Backs*. May-June, 36–37.

Dantley, M. E. (2005). African American spirituality and Cornell West's notions of prophetic pragmatism: Restructuring educational leadership in American urban schools. *Educational Administration Quarterly*, 41, 651–674.

Darder, A. (1991). *Culture and power in the classroom: A critical foundation of bicultural education.* New York, NY: Bergin & Havery.

Darder, A. (2002). *Reinventing Paulo Freire: A pedagogy of love.* Boulder, Colorado: Westview.

Darder, A. (2009). Teaching as an act of love: Reflections on Paulo Freire and his contribution to our lives and our work. In A. Darder, M. P. Barltodano & R. D. Torres (Eds.), *The critical pedagogy reader* (pp. 567–578). New York, NY: Routledge.

Day, C. (2002). School reforms and transitions in teacher professionalism and identity, *International Journal of Educational Research*, 37, 677–692.

Day, C. & Kington, A. (2008). Identity, well-being and effectiveness: The emotional contexts of teaching. *Pedagogy, Culture and Society*, 16(1), 7–23.

Dillard, C. B. (2003). Cut to heal, not to bleed: A response to Handel Wright's "An endarkened feminist epistemology?" Identity, difference and the politics of representation in educational research. *Qualitative Studies in Education*, 16(2), 227–232.

Dodson, J. E. (2007). Conceptualizations and research of African American family life in the United States. In H.P. McAdoo (Ed.), *Black families* (4th ed., pp. 51–68). Thousand Oaks: Sage.

Douglas, T.M.O. (2012). Resisting idol worship at HBCUs: The malignity of materialism, Western masculinity, and spiritual malefaction. *The Urban Review*, 44(3): 378–400.

Douglas, T. M. O., & Peck, C. M. (2013). Education by any means necessary: An historical exploration of community-based pedagogical spaces for peoples of African descent. *Educational Studies*, 49(1), 67–91.

Douglas, T.M.O. (in press). Conflicting Messages, Complex Leadership: A Critical Examination of the Influence of Sports Clubs and Neighborhoods in Leading Black Bermudian Males. Journal manuscript. *Planning & Changing.*

Fine, M., Weis, L., Weseen, S., & Wong, L. (2000). For whom? Qualitative research, representations, and social responsibilities. In N. K. Denzin & Y. S. Lincoln (eds.), *Handbook of qualitative research* (2nd ed.) (pp. 107–131). Thousand Oaks, CA: Sage Publications, Inc.

Freire, P. (1970). *Pedagogy of the oppressed.* New York: Continuum.

Freire, P. (1993). *Pedagogy of the city.* New York: Continuum.

Freire, P. (1998). *Teachers as cultural workers.* Boulder, CO: Westview Press.

Florio-Ruane, S. with de Tar, J. (2001). *Teacher education and the cultural imagination: Autobiography, conversation and narrative.* Mahweh, NJ: Lawrence Erlbaum.

Gause, C.P. (2008). *Integration matters: Navigating identity, culture, and resistance.* Peter Lang Publishing.

Giroux, H. A. (2005). *Border crossings* (2nd ed.). New York: Routledge.

Gresson, A. D. III. (2008). *Race and education primer.* New York: Peter Lang.

Hanh, T. N. (1993). *Love in action: Writings on nonviolent social change.* Berkeley, CA: Parallax Press.

Helm, B. (Ed.) (2005). Stanford Encyclopedia of Philosophy. http://plato.stanford.edu/entries/love/.

hooks, b. (1994). *Teaching to transgress: Education as the practice of freedom.* New York, NY: Routledge.

hooks, b. (2000). *Where we stand: Class matters.* New York: Routledge.

Howard, T. (2003). Culturally relevant pedagogy: Ingredients for critical teacher reflection, *Theory into Practice, 42*(3), 195–202.

Horsford, S, Grosland, T, & Gunn, K. M. (2011). *Pedagogy of the personal and professional: Toward a framework for culturally relevant leadership,* 21, 582–606.

Johnson, A. G. (2006). *Privilege, power, and difference* (2nd ed.). Boston: McGraw Hill.

Khalifa, M., Dunbar, C., & Douglas, T. M. O. (2013). Derrick Bell, CRT and educational leadership 1995-present. *Race, Ethnicity, and Education, 16*(4), 489–513.

Kincheloe, J. (2008). *Critical pedagogy* (2nd ed.). New York, NY: Peter Lang Publishing Inc.

Kincheloe, J. L, & Steinberg, S. R. (1993). A tentative description of post-formal thinking: The critical confrontation with cognitive theory. *Harvard Educational Review.* 63, 296–320.

Kincheloe, J. L, Steinberg, S. R., & Gresson III, A. D. (1996). *Measured lies.* New York: St. Martin's Press.

King, M. L. (1963). *Letter from Birmingham jail.* In H. L. Gates Jr. & N. Y. McKay (Eds.), *The Norton Anthology: African American Literature* (pp. 1854–1866). New York: W. W. Norton & Company.

Ladson-Billings, G. (1995). Toward a theory of culturally relevant pedagogy. *American Educational Research Journal.* 32(93), 465–491. Lewis, C. S. (1960). The four loves. Ireland: Harvest Books.

Loewen, J. W. (2007). *Lies my teacher told me: Everything your American history textbook got wrong.* New York: Touchstone.

McLaren, P. (2000). *Che Guevara: Paulo Freire and the pedagogy of revolution.* New York: Rowman & Littlefield.

Milner, H. R. (2000) Reflection, racial competence, and critical pedagogy: How do we prepare pre-service teachers to pose tough questions? *Race Ethnicity and Education,* 6(2), 193–208.

Montecinos, C. (2004). Paradoxes in multicultural teacher education research: students of color positioned as objects while ignored as subjects. *International Journal of Qualitative Studies in Education,* 17(2), 167–181.

Omi, M., & Winant, H. (1986). *Racial formation in the United States: From the 1960s to the 1980s.* New York: Routledge.

Palmer, P. (1998). *The courage to teach: The inner landscape of a teacher's life.* San Francisco, CA: Jossey-Bass.

Peshkin, A. (1988). In search of subjectivity—One's own. *Educational Researcher,* 17(7), 17–21.

Ryoo, J. J., Crawford, J, Moreno, D. & McLaren, P. (2009). Critical spiritual pedagogy: Reclaiming humanity through a pedagogy of integrity, community, and love. *Power and Education,* 1(1), 132–146.

Schwalbe, M. (2005). *The sociologically examined life: Pieces of the conversation.* Boston: McGraw Hill.

Sleeter, C. (2001). Preparing teachers for culturally diverse schools: Research and the overwhelming presence of whiteness. *Journal of Teacher Education,* 52(2), 94–106.

Sloan, K. (2009). Dialoguing towards a racialized identity: A necessary first step in politics of recognition. In P. M. Jenlink & F. H. Townes (Eds.). *The struggle for identity in today's schools: Cultural recognition in a time of increasing diversity* (pp. 30–48). Lanham, MD: Rowman & Littlefield.

Taylor, E., Tisdell, J. E. & Hanley, S.M. The role of teaching for critical consciousness: Implications for Adult Education Retrieved August 5, 2008 from ... http://www.edst.educ.ubc.ca/aerc/2000/tayloreetal1-final.PDF.

Villaverde, L. (2008). *Feminist primer.* New York: Peter Lang.

Walkington, J. (2005). Becoming a teacher: encouraging development of teacher identity through reflective practice. *Asia-Pacific Journal of Teacher Education,* 33(1), 53–64.

West, C. (1982). *Prophecy deliverance: An Afro-American revolutionary Christianity.* Philadelphia: Westminster Press.

West, C. (1993). *Race matters.* Boston: Beacon.

Wilson, C. M., Douglas, T. M. O., & Nganga, C. (2013). Starting with African American success: A strengths-based approach to transformative educational leadership. In L.C. Tillman & J. J. Scheurich (Eds.), *Handbook of research on educational leadership for diversity and equity.* (pp. 111–133). New York, N.Y.: Routledge/Taylor and Francis.

Zeichner, K. M. (1983). Alternative paradigms of teacher education. *Journal of Teacher Education,* 34(3), 3–9.

Zeichner, K. (1993). *Educating teachers for cultural diversity* (Special Report). East Lansing, MI: National Center for Research on Teacher Learning.

Zeichner, K., & Liston, D. (1990). Traditions of reform in U.S. teacher education. *Journal of Teacher Education,* 41(2), 3–20.

Christine and I hold similar beliefs as it relates to navigating the nuances of our positionalities, epistemology, and enacting radical love in our classrooms—namely, through building community, creating dialogic spaces, critical reflective practice, demonstrating a sincere respect for humanity and the world. For the sake of offering a broader context for considering how positionality and radical love intersect, I have focused less on my identity/experiences as a scholar with an international background. Instead, I have chosen to build on the foundation Christine has established in order to share other ways that radical love informs my praxis, rather than simply echoing her sentiments.

Admittedly, the ways in which Christine and I experience our internationalized identities (and specifically, our blackness) in the classroom are not identical. For example,

I have found that my Bermudian accent—which much like Bermuda's geopolitical history, is a unique blend of English, Caribbean, and American culture—is often privileged over many other Caribbean or African accents. I often suggest to my students that the privileging of my accent may be rooted in the fact that the Bermudian accent sounds more British than African, and is thus more aligned with a Eurocentric paradigm. Raising this point in our class discussions gives my students the opportunity to unpack how we stereotype and judge others based on the accoutrements of appearance and accents. Students from the South often confess their own prejudices about Northern accents and Northerners often speak about common perceptions of the "southern drawl." Ultimately, these discussions give students opportunities to interrogate who is perceived as intelligent, who are the insiders, who are the marginalized, and what/whose standards or norms are used to make these determinations?

Whether or not students are afraid of me because I am a Black man is not an argument that I will take up at this time. Though most students admit that I am the first Black male instructor that they have had in university (and some in their entire schooling experience), it is not always clear to me how this particular aspect of my positionality affects how my students view me. After I introduce myself and—via my different accent—destabilize the assumption that I am an African American Black man, interesting opportunities begin to open up that I gladly employ in order to probe some of the intra-cultural dynamics of identity.

Reading 5

White Privilege
Unpacking the Invisible Knapsack

Peggy McIntosh

THROUGH WORK TO BRING MATERIALS FROM Women's Studies into the rest of the curriculum, I have often noticed men's unwillingness to grant that they are over-privileged, even though they may grant that women are disadvantaged. They may say they will work to improve women's status, in the society, the university, or the curriculum, but they can't or won't support the idea of lessening men's. Denials which amount to taboos surround the subject of advantages white men gain from women's disadvantages. These denials protect male privilege from being fully acknowledged, lessened or ended.

Thinking through unacknowledged male privilege as a phenomenon, I realized that since hierarchies in our society are interlocking, there was most likely a phenomenon of white privilege which was similarly denied and protected. As a white person, I realized I had been taught about racism as something which puts others at a disadvantage, but had been taught not to see one of its corollary aspects, white privilege, which puts me at an advantage.

I think whites are carefully taught not to recognize white privilege, as males are taught not to recognize male privileges. So I have begun in an untutored way to ask what it is like to have white privilege. I have come to see white privilege as an invisible package of unearned assets which I can count on cashing in each day, but about which I was 'meant' to remain oblivious. White privilege is like an invisible weightless knapsack of special provisions, maps, passports, codebooks, visas, clothes, tools and blank checks.

Describing white privilege makes one newly accountable. As we in Women's Studies work to reveal male privilege and ask men to give up some of their power,

Peggy McIntosh, "White Privilege: Unpacking the Invisible Knapsack," *Peace and Freedom Magazine*, July/August, pp. 10-12. Copyright © 1989 by Peggy McIntosh. Reprinted with permission.

so one who writes about having white privilege must ask, "Having described it, what will I do [to lessen] or end it?"

After I realized the extent to which men work from a base of unacknowledged privilege, I understood that much of their oppressiveness was unconscious. Then I remembered the frequent charges from women of color that white women whom they encounter are oppressive. I began to understand why we are justly seen as oppressive, even when we don't see ourselves that way. I began to count the ways in which I enjoy unearned skin privilege and have been conditioned into oblivion about its existence.

My schooling gave me no training in seeing myself as an oppressor, as an unfairly advantaged person, or as a participant in a damaged culture. I was taught to see myself as an individual whose moral state depended on her individual moral will. My schooling followed the pattern my colleague Elizabeth Minnich has pointed out: whites are taught to think of their lives as morally neutral, normative, and average, and also ideal, so that when we work to benefit others, this is seen as work which will allow "them" to be more like "us."

I decided to try to work on myself at least by identifying some of the daily effects of white privilege in my life. I have chosen those conditions which I think in my case *attach somewhat more to skin-color privilege* than to class, religion, ethnic status, or geographical location, though of course all these other factors are intricately intertwined. As far as I can see, my African American co-workers, friends and acquaintances with whom I come into daily or frequent contact in this particular time, place, and line of work cannot count on most of these conditions.

1. I can if I wish arrange to be in the company of people of my race most of the time.
2. If I should need to, I can be pretty sure of renting or purchasing housing in an area which I can afford and in which I would want to live.
3. I can be pretty sure that my neighbors in such a location will be neutral or pleasant to me.
4. I can go shopping alone most of the time, pretty well assured that I will not be followed or harassed.
5. I can turn on the television or open to the front page of the paper and see people of my race widely represented.
6. When I am told about our national heritage or about "civilization," I am shown that people of my color made it what it is.
7. I can be sure that my children will be given curricular materials that testify to the existence of their race.
8. If I want to, I can be pretty sure of finding a publisher for this piece on white privilege.

9. I can go into a music shop and count on finding the music of my race represented, into a supermarket and find the staple foods which fit with my cultural traditions, into a hairdresser's shop and find someone who can cut my hair.
10. Whether I use checks, credit cards, or cash, I can count on my skin color not to work against the appearance of financial reliability.
11. I can arrange to protect my children most of the time from people who might not like them.
12. I can swear, or dress in second hand clothes, or not answer letters, without having people attribute these choices to the bad morals, the poverty, or the illiteracy of my race.
13. I can speak in public to a powerful male group without putting my race on trial.
14. I can do well in a challenging situation without being called a credit to my race.
15. I am never asked to speak for all the people of my racial group.
16. I can remain oblivious to the language and customs of persons of color who constitute the world's majority without feeling in my culture any penalty for such oblivion.
17. I can criticize our government and talk about how much I fear its policies and behavior without being seen as a cultural outsider.
18. I can be pretty sure that if I ask to talk to "the person in charge," I will be facing a person of my race.
19. If a traffic cop pulls me over or if the IRS audits my tax return, I can be sure I haven't been singled out because of my race.
20. I can easily buy posters, postcards, picture books, greeting cards, dolls, toys, and children's magazines featuring people of my race.
21. I can go home from most meetings of organizations I belong to feeling somewhat tied in, rather than isolated, out-of-place, outnumbered, unheard, held at a distance, or feared.
22. I can take a job with an affirmative action employer without having co-workers on the job suspect that I got it because of race.
23. I can choose public accommodation without fearing that people of my race cannot get in or will be mistreated in the places I have chosen.
24. I can be sure that if I need legal or medical help, my race will not work against me.
25. If my day, week, or year is going badly, I need not ask of each negative episode or situation whether it has racial overtones.
26. I can choose blemish cover or bandages in "flesh" color and have them more or less match my skin.

I repeatedly forgot each of the realizations on this list until I wrote it down. For me white privilege has turned out to be an elusive and fugitive subject. The pressure to avoid it is great, for in facing it I must give up the myth of meritocracy. If these things are true, this is not such a free country; one's life is not what one makes it; many doors open for certain people through no virtues of their own.

In unpacking this invisible knapsack of white privilege, I have listed conditions of daily experience which I once took for granted. Nor did I think of any of these perquisites as bad for the holder. I now think that we need a more finely differentiated taxonomy of privilege, for some of these varieties are only what one would want for everyone in a just society, and others give license to be ignorant, oblivious, arrogant and destructive.

I see a pattern running through the matrix of white privilege, a pattern of assumptions which were passed on to me as a white person. There was one main piece of cultural turf; it was my own turf, and I was among those who could control the turf. *My skin color was an asset for any move I was educated to want to make.* I could think of myself as belonging in major ways, and of making social systems work for me. I could freely disparage, fear, neglect, or be oblivious to anything outside of the dominant cultural forms. Being of the main culture, I could also criticize it fairly freely.

In proportion as my racial group was being made confident, comfortable, and oblivious, other groups were likely being made not confident, uncomfortable, and alienated. Whiteness protected me from many kinds of hostility, distress, and violence, which I was being subtly trained to visit in turn upon people of color.

For this reason, the word "privilege" now seems to me misleading. We usually think of privilege as being a favored state, whether earned or conferred by birth or luck. Yet some of the conditions I have described here work to systematically overempower certain groups. Such privilege simply *confers dominance* because of one's race or sex.

I want, then, to distinguish between earned strength and unearned power conferred systematically. Power from unearned privilege can look like strength when it is in fact permission to escape or to dominate. But not all of the privileges on my list are inevitably damaging. Some, like the expectation that neighbors will be decent to you, or that your race will not count against you in court, should be the norm in a just society. Others, like the privilege to ignore less powerful people, distort the humanity of the holders as well as the ignored groups.

We might at least start by distinguishing between positive advantages which we can work to spread, and negative types of advantages which unless rejected will always reinforce our present hierarchies. For example, the feeling that one belongs within the human circle, as Native Americans say, should not be seen as privilege for a few. Ideally it is an *unearned entitlement*. At present, since only a few have it, it is an *unearned advantage* for them. This paper results from a process of coming to see that some of the power which I originally saw as attendant on being a human being in the U.S. consisted in *unearned advantage and conferred dominance*.

I have met very few men who are truly distressed about systemic, unearned male advantage and conferred dominance. And so one question for me and others like me is whether we will be like them, or whether we will get truly distressed, even outraged, about unearned race advantage and conferred dominance and if so, what we will do to lessen them. In any case, we need to do more work in identifying how they actually affect our daily lives. Many, perhaps most, of our white students in the U.S. think that racism doesn't affect them because they are not people of color; they do not see "whiteness" as a racial identity. In addition, since race and sex are not the only advantaging systems at work, we need similarly to examine the daily experience of having age advantage, or ethnic advantage, or physical ability, or advantage related to nationality, religion, or sexual orientation.

Difficulties and dangers surrounding the task of finding parallels are many. Since racism, sexism, and heterosexism are not the same, the advantaging associated with them should not be seen as the same. In addition, it is hard to disentangle aspects of unearned advantage which rest more on social class, economic class, race, religion, sex and ethnic identity that on other factors. Still, all of the oppressions are interlocking, as the Combahee River Collective Statement of 1977 continues to remind us eloquently.

One factor seems clear about all of the interlocking oppressions. They take both active forms which we can see and embedded forms which as a member of the dominant group one is taught not to see. In my class and place, I did not see myself as a racist because I was taught to recognize racism only in individual acts of meanness by members of my group, never in invisible systems conferring unsought racial dominance on my group from birth.

Disapproving of the systems won't be enough to change them. I was taught to think that racism could end if white individuals changed their attitudes. [But] a "white" skin in the United States opens many doors for whites whether or not we approve of the way dominance has been conferred on us. Individual acts can palliate, but cannot end, these problems.

To redesign social systems we need first to acknowledge their colossal unseen dimensions. The silences and denials surrounding privilege are the key political tool here. They keep the thinking about equality or equity incomplete, protecting unearned advantage and conferred dominance by making these taboo subjects. Most talk by whites about equal opportunity seems to me now to be about equal opportunity to try to get into a position of dominance while denying that *systems* of dominance exist.

It seems to me that obliviousness about white advantage, like obliviousness about male advantage, is kept strongly acculturated in the United States so as to maintain the myth of meritocracy, the myth that democratic choice is equally available to all. Keeping most people unaware that freedom of confident action is there for just a small number of people props up those in power, and serves to keep power in the hands of the same groups that have most of it already.

Though systemic change takes many decades, there are pressing questions for me and I imagine for some others like me if we raise our daily consciousness on the perquisites of being light-skinned. What will we do with such knowledge? As we know from watching men, it is an open question whether we will choose to use unearned advantage to weaken hidden systems of advantage, and whether we will use any of our arbitrarily-awarded power to try to reconstruct power systems on the broader base.

Reading 6

Education by Any Means Necessary

Peoples of African Descent and Community-Based Pedagogical Spaces

Ty-Ron M. O. Douglas and Craig Peck

Across the Black Diaspora, the history of education reflects the legacy of struggle, sacrifice, and oppression that has also come to characterize significant elements of the Black experience (Anderson 1988; Branch 1988; Du Bois 1973; Morris 2009; Ogbu 2007; Woodson 1911). In fact, schooling and education for Black people have historically been two separate experiences that intersect, at times, but always continue to function independently of each other (Shujaa 1994). Systemic oppression—in forms such as slavery; racially discriminatory laws; and segregated, inequitably funded schooling—has separated Black people from school-based educational opportunities available to many members of the dominant race. This reality has caused peoples of African descent to exercise creative means of gaining access to education through the utilization of community-based pedagogical spaces. Traditionally and today, the Black Diaspora has achieved education by any means necessary through accessing a variety of learning spaces outside schools, including families, churches, and music.

This [reading] pursues an answer to our framing research question: *How and why have peoples of African descent utilized community-based pedagogical spaces outside schools?* Employing a theoretical framework that fuses historical methodology and border-crossing theory, the authors review existing scholarship, as well as primary documents, to present an historical examination of how peoples of African descent have fought for and even redefined education in learning spaces outside schools. We focus in particular on two spaces—the Black church

---

Ty-Ron Michael Douglas and Craig Peck, "Education by Any Means Necessary: Peoples of African Descent and Community-Based Pedagogical Spaces," *Educational Studies: Journal of the American Educational Studies Association*, vol. 49, no. 1, pp. 67–91. Copyright © 2013 by Taylor & Francis Group. Reprinted with permission.

and Black barbershops—that have served educative purposes. These findings inform the authors' analysis of results from an oral history project they conducted into how Black Bermudian men utilized nonschool institutions, such as the Black church, the family, and athletics clubs, to augment their personal and scholastic development.

Before proceeding, it is necessary to define and clarify a few key terms used in this article. For stylistic variety, we use several phrases interchangeably to describe nonschool-based locales, institutions, forces, or methods that serve educational purposes, including *community-based pedagogical spaces*, *learning spaces outside schools*, and *nonschool educative venues*. The phrases *peoples of African descent* and *Black people(s)* will also be used interchangeably, to recognize the diversity and plurality of Black identity as a global construct. At times, we make specific references to the *Black Diaspora* and its subcultures (for example, African American, Black Bermudian, or Black Caribbean people) but these references and descriptors are to be considered within the context and understanding of the complexities, similarities, and differences of Black identity development and not as attempts to reify the tendency to oversimplify people and the labels (mis)used to describe them (Douglas 2012a, 2013). This acknowledgement is necessary to account for our propensity to engage in regionalized, nationalistic discussions of identity that truncate discourses around the global dynamics of culture, in general, and Black identity, in particular. It is significant to note that understandings of Black identity and the education of Black people(s) must account for the interconnectedness of Blackness in a global context. Certainly the disproportionalities that plague Black people in various jurisdictions necessitate the utilization of theoretical approaches that account for Africanness/Blackness as identities that have been contested and required to cross borders, in the schoolhouse and beyond (Douglas 2012a, 2012b, 2013).

Our work compels readers to consider the history of education for Black people as one that has consistently occurred outside of schools. Based on our historical and empirical research findings, we argue that educational actors (including teachers, administrators, policy makers, and researchers) focused on seemingly school-based issues like the academic achievement gap would do well to recognize the impact that learning spaces outside of schools may have on student scholastic success, particularly for minority men. Possible solutions to vexing social issues such as poverty may, in fact, lie in the propensity that peoples of African descent have historically shown to cross institutional borders and access, as well as create nonschool-based educative venues as a means to help their culture educate and liberate, and their people survive and thrive. Equally noteworthy is the reality that every lesson learned in community-based pedagogical spaces is not positive. The animating pedagogy in these venues may, in fact, provide debilitating instruction that is devoid of necessary counternarratives to destructive, mainstream discourses on people of African descent. Rather than thriving, some individuals may experience lives of deprivation, in part because of the life lessons they received in spaces that, for others, have been sources of resistance.

Theoretical Framework

Our theoretical framework incorporates historical methodology and border crossing theory as related to education and peoples of African descent. Toward historical methodology, this [reading] follows in a tradition of scholarship that has examined how populations in general, and peoples of African descent specifically, have pursued education outside schools. Freire (1993), for example, proposed a "pedagogy of the oppressed" to occur outside of state-controlled schools (1). Of importance also is Cremin (1970, 1980, 1988), a major three-volume history that defined education as "the deliberate, systematic, and sustained effort to transmit, evoke, or acquire knowledge, attitudes, skills, or sensibilities" (1970, xiii). The history of education for Black people is, in fact, one that has consistently occurred outside of traditional schooling and within alternative educative venues such as families (Billingsley 1992), churches (Billingsley 1999; Billingsley and Caldwell 1991; Douglas 2012b; Hale 2001; Martin and McAdoo 2007), barbershops (Franklin 1985; Harris-Lacewell and Mills 2004; Mills 2005, 2006), social protest groups (Carson 1995; Peck 2001; Perlstein 2002) and music (Alim 2011; Lipsitz 1994; Morrell and Duncan-Andrade 2002).

The reality that learning occurs outside of schools is not lost on many individuals within Black communities. For example, the term *educated fool* is commonly used in Black communities to describe people who have been schooled within mainstream structures but lack the cultural relevancy or *street smarts* to be effective agents for and within their communities (Shujaa 1994). This language is rooted in the understanding within Black communities that traditional schooling experiences alone are not sufficient for preparing and, in effect, educating Black people for life, resiliency, and service.

In regard to the oral history aspect of our project, this [reading] builds on the strong oral tradition of Bermudian culture (Zuill 1978), as well as the social, political, cultural, and economic ties that Bermuda holds with the United States, England, Canada, and the Caribbean (Douglas 2012a; Douglas and Gause 2009; Hodgson 2008). These ties are reflected in the dismal statistics of academic displacement for Black Bermudian men that mirror the challenges faced by Black men in the aforementioned countries. The role of nonschool-based pedagogical spaces for Black people in Bermuda has garnered more interest since the publication of a study (Mincy, Jethwani-Keyser, and Haldane 2009) that confirmed that over 50% of Black men in Bermuda fail to graduate from the public school system. Furthermore, we agree with Hodgson (2008), who contends that "the Black Bermudian experience has frequently shadowed the Black American experience" (4).

Ironically, national data on the education of Black children in the United States reveal equally disturbing statistics of disproportionality: African American children are 50% more likely not to finish high school than White children; African American children are also the population most likely to be funneled to special education programs, and the least likely to be identified for gifted and talented programs (Children's Defense Fund 2007; Douglas and Gause 2009; Wilson, Douglas, and Nganga, in press). These findings seem to be consistent with the experiences of Black men in other jurisdictions (Douglas and Gause 2009). For example, studies on Black Caribbean men in the United Kingdom also report significant educational and vocational disadvantages and disproportionalities for Black men (Fitzgerald, Finch, and Nove 2000; Gilborn and Mirza 2000; Graham and Robinson 2004; Sewell 1997; Wrench and Hassan 1996).

Besides attention to the history of education among peoples of African descent, our theoretical framework also expressly incorporates border theory. A single definition cannot fully capture the fluidity, breadth, and transience of border theory. In fact, there are many means, mediums, and modes that border theory/theorists can use to engage in their critical work of rupturing dominant positionalities and deconstructing vestiges of the colonial/postcolonial and center/periphery binarisms (Douglas 2012a, 2013). Manifestations of border theory include, as Hicks (1991) explains, "border writing," "border text," "border subject," and "border culture," which embrace the transformational power of border positionalities and "polarities" to challenge hierarchies and complex power dynamics (xvi). Similarly, Giroux (2005) utilizes the concept of *border pedagogy* to describe the power relations in educative settings that must be dismantled by students and teachers—acting essentially as border crossers—who are willing to challenge the "physical ... [and] cultural borders historically constructed and socially organized within rules and regulations that limit and enable particular identities, individual capacities, and social forms" (22). What some border theorists have in common is the belief that voices and identities live and are silenced within, across, and on geopolitical, socio-cultural and institutional boundaries and borders (Anzaldua 2007; Giroux 2005; Hicks 1991). The significance of border theory for challenging colonial/postcolonial binarisms in this study is enhanced by the fact that Bermuda is still a colony of England and border crossing (both literally and figuratively) to other jurisdictions is particularly valuable for residents of a 21-square-mile island in the middle of the Atlantic Ocean. The data collected as part of this study supports this claim.

Methods and Data Sources
Analysis of Historical Primary and Secondary Sources

Following a methodological approach similar to that of historians such as Anderson (1988) and Tyack and Cuban (1995), we utilize existing historical scholarship (*secondary sources*) as well as what historians call *primary source* documents (for instance, newspaper articles, organizational documents, or autobiographies) to establish an interpretive, analytical overview regarding how and why African peoples have utilized community-based pedagogical spaces. We focus in particular on two spaces—the Black church and the Black barbershop—that have played a sustained educational role. We supplement our discussion of themes identified in existing scholarship by referencing primary sources, especially first-person narratives of various types. In doing so, we hope to give voice to times past by including quotes from those who lived it.

Oral History

The participants in the oral history aspect of the study are Black Bermudian men. We used network sampling (Wolff 1999) to recruit the four participants, who ranged in age from 30 to 70 years old. During the initial interview, we asked them an open-ended, grand narrative question: "Tell me the story of your life" (see Casey 1993). Like Thompson (1978), we believe that "oral history gives history back to the people in their own words. And in giving a past, it also helps them towards a future of their own making" (226). In addition, we determined that the grand narrative question would allow the subjects an opportunity to freely prioritize the educative spaces—schools or otherwise—that were most significant and meaningful in their lives. We conducted a follow-up interview with each participant to give them the opportunity to elaborate on particular topics and clarify any ideas raised during their initial interview; this follow-up interview was also used for the purposes of member checking. All individual names of participants, associates, and neighborhoods used in this [reading] are pseudonyms to protect the confidentiality and anonymity of our respondents.

We analyzed the oral histories of the participants using thematic analysis as outlined by Glesne (2006). The steps of the thematic analysis process were (a) collecting data, (b) coding and categorizing the data, (c) searching and synthesizing for patterns, and (d) interpreting the data. Using this method revealed themes that emerged from our participants' responses to the questions, as well as connections to the historical literature we reviewed. We established interrater reliability in the coding process by codetermining the codes to be used in analyzing the data. From the initial round of interviews, we analyzed the first transcript together and then analyzed the final three transcriptions separately. We then compared our individual coding of the three transcriptions, discussed similarities and differences, and came to consensus on the interpretation of the data. We analyzed the data from the follow-up interviews individually, highlighting specific statements and topics of particular relevance to community-based pedagogical spaces.

Findings and Analysis

Learning Spaces Outside Schools: An Historical Overview

Throughout their history, members of the Black Diaspora have produced a strong heritage of accessing education through community-based pedagogical spaces. For instance, previous scholars have demonstrated how slaves in the American South established educational networks within plantations and used clever subterfuge to learn to read. They did so often at significant personal and collective risk, especially by the mid-1800s, as high profile slave revolts led by literate slaves cemented, in slave owners' minds, a clear correlation: a slave's quest for knowledge was a quest for liberty. Some Southern states, in fact, established laws that made the education of slaves a heavily punishable offense and enforced illiteracy through intimidation and violence (Cornelius 1983; Webber 1978; Williams 2005). A freed Georgia slave reported, "If they caught you trying to write, they would cut your finger off and if they caught you again they would cut your head off" (Cornelius 1983, 174). The Puritan background of some White slave masters in 1600s and 1700s Bermuda compelled them to encourage Bible-reading abilities in slaves. However, Black Bermudian slaves used creative means to assert their literacy in ways that extended beyond Bible study, including occasions in which they "turned the tables on their White masters by adopting the very method Englishmen had traditionally approved: the written petition" to formally request freedom (Bernhard 1999, 276).

Reflecting on his quest for literacy and liberty, the former slave turned abolitionist leader Frederick Douglass, in his 1845 autobiography, remembered the power and purpose of slave owners' attempts to enforce a regime of "mental darkness" (Douglass 1995, 22). Douglass recalled his master once stating, "Now, if you teach that nigger (speaking of myself) how to read there would be no keeping him. It would forever unfit him to be a slave. He would at once become unmanageable, and of no value to his master" (20). Such a statement only emboldened Douglass to find alternative means of learning. He explained, "though conscious of the difficulty of learning without a teacher, I set out with high hope, and a fixed purpose, at whatever cost of trouble, to learn how to read" (20). He recalled that he learned to write by learning a few basic letters, and then challenging White boys in the street to top his abilities. As these other boys frantically scribbled letters to best their competitor, Douglass was exposed to and learned more. "During this time, my copy book was the board fence, brick wall, and pavement; my pen and ink was a lump of chalk" (26). Douglass also reveals how, much like the Bermudian slaves, he was able to write for himself and others a false pass to freedom by using the reading and writing skills he had developed under the tutelage of his slave-master's wife (Douglass 1995). Frederick Douglass embodied a slave culture that encouraged seeking education by any means necessary.

Historians have demonstrated how, though slavery had ended in the post-Civil War segregated American South, educational opportunities for African Americans were severely limited (Anderson 1988, Fultz 1995). Author Richard Wright, who grew up within those conditions, described in his autobiography how he gleaned much of his education outside of schools. He remembered,

> At the age of twelve, before I had one full year of formal schooling, I had a conception of life that no experience would ever erase, a predilection for what was real that no argument could ever gainsay, a sense of the world that was mine and mine alone, a notion as to what life meant that no education could ever alter, a conviction that the meaning of living came only when one was struggling to wring a meaning out of meaningless suffering. (Wright, 1945, 87–88)

His early-life classroom, in fact, included nonschool educative venues such as family and church, as well as neighborhoods suffused with relentless, White-dominated race relations. Importantly, these venues were not always conducive to positive lessons. Wright, for instance, told his grandmother at one point, "that old church of yours is messing up my life!" (126). Wright recognized life experience as an ambivalent teacher, explaining, "At the age of twelve I had an attitude toward life that was to endure ... that was to make me skeptical of everything while seeking everything, tolerant of all and yet critical" and a "spirit" that "made me strangely tender and cruel, violent and peaceful" (88). Such were the imperfect, yet sustaining, educational tensions of a life learned outside of schools.

As the struggle for Black freedom emerged to challenge overt racist oppression, protest groups engaged in social justice efforts that relied upon essential instructional elements. From 1961 to 1966 in the American South, the Student Non-violent Coordinating Committee (SNCC) used participatory workshops to introduce community members to nonviolent tactics. As historian Clayborne Carson (1995) demonstrated, the organization put these lessons into practice through sit-ins and taught *freedom songs* that served as a binding emotional force. SNCC freedom schools provided free instruction to students poorly served in segregated schools (Perlstein 1990), and media coverage of the SNCC freedom schools instructed the broader nation that powerful change was underway in the American South. A 1964 profile in the widely distributed *New York Times Sunday Magazine*, for instance, described a Mississippi freedom school political education session in which adult African American women discussed the potential benefits of gaining the right to vote, with one woman stating, "We could elect some Negroes in office." Another woman explained further, "Some could be sheriff. Some could be judge. Some could ... could maybe be president" (Watters 1964, 43). In the later Civil Rights

Movement era, the Black Panther Party used an array of institutions and initiatives, including their newspaper, schools, and use of mass media coverage, to deliver political education to a vast and varied audience (Peck 2001; Perlstein 2002). Black Panther founder Huey Newton noted, "The main purpose of a vanguard group [like the Black Panthers] should be to raise the consciousness of the masses through educational programs and certain activities the party will participate in" (Newton, 1968, 42–43). Black Panther co-founder Bobby Seale explained, "We go through a long process of trying to educate the people. All of them. The hippies, Whites, Blacks, everybody. We try to organize them" (Seale 1991, 251).

Suggesting how the pursuit of education outside schools crossed borders, the Black Panther Party cited Frantz Fanon's *Wretched of the Earth* (1963) as a seminal source regarding the proper approach to revolution (see, for instance, Newton 1968). Fanon stressed the essential importance of political education, broadly construed, to Black freedom efforts in Algeria. He stated, "Political education means opening up the mind, awakening the mind, and introducing it to the world. It is as Cèsaire said: 'To invent the souls of men'" (Fanon 1963, 138). The Black Power Movement of the late 1960s and 1970s was also vibrant and impactful in Bermuda due to the influence of activists like the Black Beret Cadre and Pauulu Kamarakafego. According to Bermudian historian Swan (2009), the meaningful relationships that were sustained between Bermudian activists and "revolutionary organizations across the African Diaspora such as the Black Panthers," are emblematic of the strong and steady "voice of Black [Bermudian] dissent" that could often be heard amongst the bellows of Black activists from "the wider Black world" (xi). For example, John Hilton Bassett Jr., "the long standing chief of staff" of the Black Beret Cadre, "raised money by writing and producing plays" and much like "activities organized by the Black Panthers, he used the funds to feed the needy in the Black community" (Swan 2009, 98–99). In these respects, Black Bermudians have not only tapped into the tradition of accessing community-based pedagogical spaces for peoples of African descent, but they have also crossed borders by remaining connected to the larger struggles for political, social, and economic uplift for peoples across the Black Diaspora.

Over the last several centuries, music forms such as spirituals, work songs, and jazz spread across the Diaspora and instructed generations of Black peoples (Charters 2009). In the mid-20th century, jazz icon Billie Holiday sang "Strange Fruit," a song whose haunting melody and stark lyrics ("Black body swinging in the Southern breeze/Strange fruit hanging from the poplar trees") offered a soul-scorching protest against lynchings in the American South (Margolick 2000). Today, hip-hop music crosses borders as a powerful influence on Black and other minority youth and cultures throughout the world (Alim 2011; Gause 2008). Some scholars have advocated bringing hip-hop into the classroom as a means to more effectively engage students who have struggled in traditional academic structures (Hill 2009; Morrell and Duncan-Andrade 2002; Runell and Diaz 2007; Stovall 2006). Hip-hop artists have consciously accepted and presented their role as cultural instructors. Boogie Down Productions, for instance, released an album *Edutainment* with a title that accurately reflected the collaborative's twin goals of entertaining the Black community while also educating it about prevailing social issues (Boogie Down Productions 1990). Similarly, the history and educative power of other musical genres, like Negro spirituals (Lovell 1939) and Afro-Caribbean reggae music (Manuel, Bilby, and Largey 2006), affirm that education through music has been utilized across the Black Diaspora.

Learning Spaces Outside Schools: Focus on the Black Church

Spirituality has been an ever-present and consistently influential force in Black communities (Dantley 2005; Martin and McAdoo 2007; McAdoo 2007). As the preeminent institution for the expression of spirituality among peoples of African descent, the Black church has been historically active as a socializing space and support system (Evans 2008; Frey and Wood, 1998; Hale 2001; Lincoln and Mamiya 1990; Turner and Bagley 2000). The centrality of spirituality and religion for peoples of African descent is a nexus for the diverse cultures reflected in African, Caribbean, South American, and African American people, whose ancestors "relied upon an African-based understanding of life, death, and creation to help them adjust to an unpredictable social environment" (McAdoo 2007, 98). Drawing on African patterns of "multigenerational" interconnectivity and the "fictive kin (nonrelatives who are as close and involved in the family as blood relatives)" (McAdoo 2007, 98), the Black Church has served as a buffer and bridge for the sustenance and uplift of Black people. More than that, as Hale (2001) asserts, "the African American church is the most important institution in the African American community and is supported and controlled entirely by African American people. African American churches were burned and bombed during and after the modern civil rights movement because they represented black power, independence, and self-determination" (155). Serving as a space where spirituality and education converge, the Black church has been and continues to be a reservoir and resource for educational advancement for Black people. C. Eric Lincoln noted, "Beyond its purely religious function, as critical as that function has been, the Black church in its historical role as lyceum, conservatory, forum, social service center, political academy and financial institution has been and is for Black America the mother of our culture, the champion of our freedom, the hallmark of our civilization" (Lincoln 1989; quoted in Billingsley 1992, 354, and Putnam 2000, 68–69).

Scholars (e.g., Billingsley and Caldwell 1991; Lincoln and Mamiya 1990) have acknowledged that educational outreach programs have been a top priority for many Black churches, including tutoring initiatives, preschool/day care, GED programs, and private elementary schools. Notably, the educational focus of Black churches is not new. From its inception, the mission of the Black Sabbath/Sunday School was to promote literacy amongst slaves, newly freed African people, and (later) young people who had not been prepared for college admission (Hale 2001). The interactive relationship between spirituality and education for African Americans is evident in the fact that when many historically Black colleges were founded, Sunday schools were also established and faculty members were obligated to serve as Sunday school teachers as well (Hale 2001). Similarly, the Black church has been an educational, oratorical, and artistic training ground for everyday citizens and contemporary artists alike. Lincoln and Mamiya (1990) assert that "Black churches have served as concert halls, art galleries, and public forums, and the first public performance seen or given by many Black children often occurred in church" (312). The scholars note further that "special Sunday services were set aside for the participation of children and children's choirs on 'Children's Day,' or 'junior church' occasions" (312).

Narratives from history demonstrate the centrality of education in the churches of the Black Diaspora, though the institution's role in serving its people may have changed over time. In the United States in 1898, for instance, African American evangelist Samuel Robert Cassius sought to fuse teaching and religion through the establishment of an Oklahoma industrial school modeled after Booker T. Washington's Tuskegee Institute. He explained, "The negro's mind can be changed in but one way; that is, to educate both mind and hands," with an end goal of producing "the great industrial army of tomorrow" (Cassius 1898, 39). As a result, Cassius asserted, "you produce a happy, independent people, who will be a credit to the nation and a safe guard to the republic" (Cassius 1898, 39). More than seventy years later, seminarian Major J. Jones (1971) offered a starkly different message in proposing the recognition of a "theology of hope" closely intertwined with the ongoing struggle for Black consciousness and equality (87). He explained, "The Black man has a right to appropriate his God in his own color, and to express this in art forms, language symbols, and literature. … Indeed, when the oppressed no longer is satisfied to accept or adopt the God of the oppressor, especially his explicit or implicit color as it is expressed in art and literature, then the process of liberation has begun" (114). Recalling her childhood church experiences in early to mid-twentieth-century Bermuda, historian Ruth Thomas captures elements of a Black Bermudian church experience as a conservative worship setting where "stark white walls," "a strict moral code," "no instrumental music," and children who "understood the meaning of silence" were counterbalanced by "richly blended, melodious, muted voices" joined together "in eight-part harmony" (Jones 1993, 243). Clearly, different times and locales produced different churches with different lessons for members of the Diaspora.

Learning Spaces Outside Schools: Focus on the Black Barbershop

The Black barbershop is a powerful institution in the Black community (Harris-Lacewell and Mills 2004; Hart and Bowen 2004; Mills 2005, 2006). As a profession, business entity, and center of socialization, the Black barbershop has been a central fixture in the Black community from as early as the nineteenth century (Harris-Lacewell and Mills 2004). More than seeing their profession as a fiscal stepping stone, Black barbers used their influence and opportunities for the betterment of their community. In fact, Harris-Lacewell and Mills (2004) assert: "From slavery to freedom, barbers and hairstylists have constituted the overwhelming majority of entrepreneurs in the African American community. Both as slaves and as free men, Black barbers used both monopoly and a White consumer base to their advantage. Their profession provided them with power, prestige, and status in the Black community. These men did not use this status and wealth solely for individual gain. African American barbers often used their earnings to actively engage in uplift activities" (164).

This ethos of service and community accountability continues today through the dialogue, networking, and mentoring that takes place in many Black barbershops. As a community-based pedagogical space, the Black barbershop has become a sanctuary where Black men can find community, camaraderie, culturally relevant discourse (Douglas, 2012a; Nunley, 2011), and "meaningful everyday Black talk" (Harris-Lacewell and Mills 2004, 167). Reminiscent of the spaces that allowed slaves to communicate beyond the listening ear of slave masters, the contemporary barbershop is a socio-political space where dialogue can occur beyond the confines of the work place and the home. For many Black men, communication with employers and family members is a complex experience. Similarly, for many Black men, the Black barbershop is the only space where they will be in the company of other Black men exclusively (Harris-Lacewell and Mills 2004).

Based on a study of sex-role socialization in a Black urban barbershop, Franklin (1985) noted that topics "ranging from international crises to neighborhood ruckuses" exemplify the breadth of barbershop discourse (971). Franklin further contended that the barbershop is a powerful educational space that can both damage and empower, depending on the clientele on a particular day. Specifically, Franklin notes: (a) "Masculinity is negotiated actively by adult males and passively by male youth" in urban barbershops (976); (b) "barbershop[s] literally capture the 'minds' of Black youth for one to two hours approximately two times per month," during which time "vulnerable Black male youth are exposed to a predominantly male environment which reveals 'expectations' held for them by a cross-section of males with whom these Black male youth identify" (976); and (c) barbershop discourse provides messages of "physical aggression" and defeatism, such as stories about Black male failure due to external constraints (i.e., the White man, society) without reference to the successes of Black men (977–978). These findings suggest that those who seek to utilize the pedagogical potential of the barbershop and other community-based spaces must also acknowledge and address some of the detrimental practices and unspoken rules that exist in these spaces. Others have identified the barbershop as a powerful nonschool-educative venue (Douglas 2012a; Nunley 2011), although published studies focusing on the barbershop as a site for educational intervention research targeting African American men are scarce (Hart and Bowen 2004).

Narrative voices from history demonstrate the importance of barbershops to the culture of the Black Diaspora. One of Bermuda's premiere vocalists and orchestra leaders of the 1920s, Harry Foster, learned to play the violin, bass violin, and cello in the barbershop, while also developing barbering skills that eventually led to him opening his own barbershop (Butler 2006). In a feature printed in African-American newspapers, historian Carter G. Woodson (1932) explained, "The cause of the Race can get a hearing in the Negro barber shop more easily than in a Negro school. In the barber shop the Negro has freedom; in the school the Negro must do what somebody else wants done" (2A). In a 1961 interview, novelist Ralph Ellison stated, "There is no place like a Negro barbershop for hearing what Negroes really think. There is more unselfconscious affirmation to be found here on a Saturday than you can find in a Negro college in a month, or so it seems to me" (Stern 1961, 9). In contemporary times, the popularity of the *Barbershop* films, including the related film *Beauty Shop*, help showcase the continuing importance of the institution to Black life in the United States.

Learning Spaces Outside Schools: Oral Histories of Black Bermudians

To gain a greater understanding of how individuals of African descent have personally experienced education in learning spaces outside schools, we conducted an oral history study of four Black Bermudian men between the ages of 30 and 70. The results of the study reveal that nonschool-educative venues are impactful centers of learning, socialization, and support, and suggest that some of these community-based spaces may in fact have had a more substantial impact on the subjects' lives than schools. To provide further illustration of how our participants discussed nonschool-educative spaces, we provide brief portrayals of the educational experiences—in school and out—described by our participants.

Asked the open-ended question, "Tell me the story of your life," three of the four participants talked without interviewer prompting about the significance of Black churches in their personal development. In fact, it was not uncommon for these participants to frame their identities and personal decisions in relation to their commitment to or disengagement from the church. David, who is in his early 70s, provided an example of how the church or spirituality can serve as the beats on which the lyrics of other lived experiences (i.e., family relationships) synchronize or fall out of rhythm. He began his narrative this way:

> I was pretty much brought up in a Christian environment. At an early age I left the church and went out in the world. And I got caught up in the things that go on in the world—which are alcohol and drugs—not too much of the drug business but alcohol and I thought I was in control of it. I got married when I was 19. I was a pretty good father for many years. I went back in the church while I was married. Then I left the church again and my marriage dropped apart and I dropped apart.

In his narrative, David described his battles with alcoholism and mental illness as manifestations of his failure to commit to God. Nonetheless, though David left the church he later returned, seeing this space as an important route to revitalization. Reflecting on his life's journey and the healthy relationships he now enjoys with his children and church family, he states: "I never thought I would make it this far. When I stood up at [church name] Church and was getting ready to be baptized, I cried. It was because I never thought I would make it back there. It is dangerous when you leave like that because there is no guarantee that you will make it back. You can get snuffed out through death or whatever or just your lifestyle can do it. Praise the Lord. He saved me. My health is pretty good."

Steve, who was in his late 40s at the time of the interview, repeatedly referenced his experience being raised in a foster home, and the affinity he has for these individuals that became family to him. He stated: "I had a rough life. I was brought up by a ... foster mother on Springfield Avenue. [Ms. Smith] brought me up. She [Ms. Smith] calls me her nephew and I called her auntie. She was like a mama to me. Anyhow, she had a couple of sisters ... [and] a brother. ... They were special people." Including Steve, three of the four participants discussed—without interviewer prompting—the importance of family to their personal development, while all four mentioned relationships as a pivotal factor in their lived and learned experiences. Steve also expressly talked about spirituality within the context of his frequent hospital trips to visit family members and relationships with members of his sports club: "My cousin [at] the hospital ... gets upset when she doesn't see me. The one who had the stroke. I am going to see her tomorrow. She is coming around now [be]cause the Lord is bringing her around. Everybody needs prayer every day. Just like the boys from [the Chargers Sports Club]. [Do you know] the boy who got killed (referencing a young man who had recently been killed in a motor cycle accident)? I used to help that little boy. That was my mate. I told his brother, 'Let's keep the faith.'"

Devon was a 30-year-old participant who consistently referenced the strong influence of the neighborhood on his upbringing. Of the four participants, he most frequently mentioned the absence of strong family support during his developmental years. As a result, his community, his neighborhood peers, and "trial and error" became the most dominant teachers. Devon began his narrative by sharing the following: "I was raised on Thompson Street, Gilchrest Parish. I used to play football. I was a good footballer. … I went to Blake Secondary. I wanted to be a lot of things, like [a] lawyer and stuff like that. But then stuff happens. You go around the wrong people and stuff like that. You go the wrong way. Some people go different ways. You learn from your experiences."

Although participants like Devon consistently referenced significant learning experiences and relationships that were sustained in spaces outside of the schoolhouse, only one of the participants discussed his schooling experience in any detail without being specifically prompted to do so, and three of the four participants described their schooling in terms that suggested that it was a regrettable or negative experience. Further underscoring the centrality of nonschool-based pedagogical spaces in the lives of the Black men in our study, some participants even chose a church parking lot or the neighborhood sports/community club as the site for their interview with the researcher.

Kevin was one such participant who chose to meet in a church parking lot to conduct the interview. The son of participant David, described earlier, Kevin offers a narrative that crosses the generational borders to cast light on the distinct connections and disconnects that emerged in response to his father's struggles and triumphs. Kevin grounded his narrative in the various neighborhoods and communities that his family lived in. Kevin, now in his late 30s, stated:

> I am Bermudian born and raised. I started out my life up in Brenau Parish … on Haven Road. I was a bit too young to remember that. What I do remember is when I lived on Jewelry Road. I came up with what started off with what we would term complete family: mother, father, supportive grandparents, aunts and uncles and as time went on for various reasons the family broke. My father was removed from the home. But in doing that my mom was ensuring that we maintained a form of relationship as we could. He used to drink a lot. She would allow us to maintain contact with him in whatever way we could. We moved around a lot. On [this] 21 square mile I think I have lived in every parish at least once; some of them, 4 or 5 times.

Kevin's early years were made more difficult by the constant moving that his family did once his father was no longer in the home. But houses were not the only things that changed in Kevin's life and parish borders were not the only borders Kevin crossed as he journeyed to manhood. Although spirituality was a mainstay for most of his life, at times he struggled with what he describes as "the dichotomy of two religions" as a result of moving back and forth between two religious denominations. He declared:

> If you can find dichotomy in two religions then you can find dichotomy in your life. You can find a reason and a means and a justification for doing just about anything. When I was in my early 20s, I guess, we had a situation where financially my family, my mom, my tight family, my nuclear family didn't have a lot of finances. And we were always struggling. My mom was working 12 double shifts, you know 16-hour shifts to just put food on your table and keep a roof over our head. My family decided that, in a lot of ways, they would shield me from the realities of our situation. I grew up resenting the area that we lived in. I didn't have all the stuff that my friends had or I didn't have all the stuff that even other members of my family had access to … finances, access to getting certain types of clothes.

These dynamics, he believes, were contributing factors to his decision to involve himself in the sale of narcotics, which eventually led to a stint in prison. In fact, his prison experience was significant in him turning his life around. Reflecting upon the day of his release from jail, he says: "I remember saying to myself that there will never be a time that I will go back there [to prison]." What he did not know, however, is how his conviction and prison term would infringe upon his capacity to travel to the United States. Similarly, many Black Bermudian men have forfeited their rights to cross literal borders into foreign countries due to criminal convictions. In this regard, the 21-square-mile island that tourists have come to describe as paradise has become a 21-square-mile prison for Black men who are now chained to *the Rock*.[1] Kevin's experience in this respect is significant because it both underscores the centrality of border crossing to the Bermudian experience and it also reveals the rebirth experience of a man who is able to reconcile his personal and spiritual dichotomies:

> One thing that I didn't know … was that something … I did in my early 20s [could] still hinder me in my late 30s. In the US [Immigration Department] they have a *stop list*. They get information on the incarcerated individuals and what they have been incarcerated for and they put you on the *stop list*. And once you are on the *stop list* you can't travel from Bermuda

to the US, which is the most economical travelling spot to get to from Bermuda. If you go to London it is more expensive than Bermuda. But when you go to the States everything is cheaper. And so when I found out I was on the *stop list* my first wife and I were about to go on a well-deserved [yet delayed] honeymoon ... [but] I [was] stopped at the airport; I couldn't go. She came back early and I couldn't leave. And I remember [thinking] that my travelling career [was over] and I am trapped on 21 square miles in Bermuda for one mistake. But there was a different plan though. I started to focus my life back on God. I got baptized back into the church. I started to pray a little bit more and started to focus on more spiritual things. And a couple of years after that, which was unheard of for the amount of time and the amount of the drugs that were involved in [my] case, when I went to visit the US Immigration/Customs official to sit down ... in an unprecedented [decision] I got a waiver; I got paper work that I would be able to travel and I just go back every year to renew it and so far, even after 9–11, some of the procedures and processes have changed, I have still been able to travel to the US on a pretty consistent basis and I am very thankful for that because there are a lot of guys here that are just stuck. They can't get off the island.

Kevin's experience of having his international travel privileges restricted and revoked is not unique. Sadly, there's a disturbing frequency and irony to the reality that so many Black men are stuck in Bermuda. As policy makers and school stakeholders in Bermuda and across the world make decisions to address the achievement gap between White students and students of color,[2] the data in this study underscores the reality that spaces outside of the schoolhouse are highly impactful locales in the lives of many Black males.

In regard to the use of specific learning spaces outside schools, the participants' recollections of the barbershop provide compelling insight into the uniqueness of their experiences. For Steve, the barbershop was a bridge to another educative venue, the church: "I went there [to the barbershop] a lot. ... They taught me a lot. [One particular] barber taught me about the church—about Christianity—since it was a Christian barbershop." Kevin's enthusiastic overtures about the barbershop reveal the educative impact of the barbershop in his life:

The Black barbershop ... ha, ha, ha! That is the Black hub. ... You would go, and you would sit down, and there was no, every topic is meat for discussion in a barbershop. There is no taboo; there is nothing off limits [and] there is no situation or circumstance that's out there. You can talk sports. Sports came up. ... It was literally, if you were a Black man, that is where you were taught to debate. And how to maintain, how to give passion, without turning to violence. And that is something that our young people could use a little bit more of. You know, to sit down, you talk about religious stuff if you wanted to. Political stuff if you wanted to. And you could get as passionate and heated as you wanted. But when you left the barbershop, you and whomever you were discussing it with, would be like, 'Yeah, I check you next week Friday,' or 'Check you next week Thursday,' or whatever the case may be. It was just a perpetual place to just hang out, chill, and sometimes you would be in there sitting for hours and you didn't mind. [The barber] Mr. Clark, he always taught us guys when we were younger that when you go out, you represent more than yourself. So while you may look tore up from the floor up and think your only representing yourself, dude, when you go out, you're representing your family, you are representing your bloodline in certain ways and so for that, you need to shave, and you know, look a little bit tighter on a day to day basis. And then, when it comes to special occasions, you got to look real tight. And then the other things it taught me, it just taught me the art of agreeing to disagree. It's all right to have a difference of opinion with a person, a guy or whatever, and it didn't have to break down into a fight, a curse fest, because he didn't allow cursing in his barbershop. It taught you how to be a gentleman, as opposed to sitting off on the street you know saying 'f' this and 'f' you, drinking or whatever you did, all this other stuff. And it taught you to be a really good debater. You couldn't come into a barbershop and talk about your team without some facts and figures. You had to know what was what. It helped, it really helped.

Kevin also reported, "I get my haircut by my wife now and have been for some years, but I miss the interaction of the Black barbershop." Such a statement suggests how the venues where individuals access lessons may change over a lifetime.

Ironically, Kevin's dad, David, views the barbershop quite differently: "If a guy could cut my hair in five minutes he was my barber. My idea of a barbershop was to go get a haircut and get out of there." Devon uses remarkably similar language in describing how he approaches the barbershop: "It's a place to go get my haircut. I just want to get in and get out. [For] some people, [the barbershop is] their comfort zone where they talk about their stuff or whatever, that's not me." Whereas, for two of the participants, the barbershop is valued as an engaging learning space, the other two participants find their education elsewhere.

One more space deserves mention. Although the prison experience emerged as a motif in one of the interviews and served as a context where a subject's personal rebirth may have occurred, this occurrence may be an exception, rather than the general rule, for men who enter the penal system. Kevin's counsel is profound and summative in this regard, even as he underscores why we need to proactively employ community-based educative spaces to promote positive outcomes for Black men prior to them entering the penal system:

> A lot of people in Bermuda (who have never been to prison) think that our prison is like a country club. There are a lot of misconceptions. People think that the units are air conditioned ... [and] they [prisoners] are down there living in the lap of luxury. There's not a lick of air condition in there. The place is built with a 20-foot wall around it that is 4 feet thick. [There's] razor wire over the top. It is on the water but no water breeze comes in; unless you are on the upper floors you are not catching any breeze ... in [a] little 6-by-9 cubicle [with] your toilet, your sink, [and] your personal items. So for people who [think prisoners] keep going to prison because it is a joy ride and because their lives in there are better than the life they have outside ... [they shouldn't] think that. People keep going back [to] prison because they don't know how to do anything else. They are not equipped to handle not being in prison, and they are not able to get within what society wants them to do and so they do other things.

Implications: Considering Complexities, Connecting Dots

In the end, nonschool-based educative venues and personal lessons learned from lived experiences essentially framed the personal journeys described in the participants' narratives. The wide range of spaces/experiences discussed by the participants include: the family, neighborhoods, sports clubs, church/spirituality, barbershops, prison, jobs/work, and international travel. Particularly noteworthy are the historical connections and border-crossing roots/routes among the participants' narratives and historical accounts. For instance, much like the African American twentieth-century novelist Ralph Ellison believed "there is no place like a Negro barbershop for hearing what Negroes really think" (Stern 1961, 9), the contemporary Black Bermudian, Kevin, states, "the Black barbershop ... ha, ha, ha! That is the Black hub ... . If you were a Black man, that is where you were taught to debate." Growing up with little formal schooling in early twentieth-century American South, Richard Wright (1945) remembered: "At the age of twelve, I had an attitude toward life that was to endure ... that was to make me skeptical of everything while seeking everything, tolerant of all and yet critical" and a "spirit" that "made me strangely tender and cruel, violent and peaceful" (88). Across time and geographic space, our study participant, Devon, remembers the educational effects of growing up in a 1980s Bermudian neighborhood: "I was raised on Thompson Street, Gilchrest Parish. ... I wanted to be a lot of things, like [a] lawyer and stuff like that. But then stuff happens. You go around the wrong people. ... You go the wrong way. ... You learn from your experiences." Spanning time and crossing borders, life has not always been an easy teacher.

Complexities abound in trying to understand the implications of our findings regarding community-based pedagogical spaces. Fundamental questions remain, such as: Can community-based pedagogical spaces be utilized beyond the manner in which they are presently employed? Should community-based pedagogical spaces be utilized more extensively than they are presently employed? How can we utilize community-based pedagogical spaces without compromising the authenticity of the spaces?

In answering these questions, we need to think carefully about how we ultimately approach educational interventions in community spaces. There are many borders still to be crossed and dots to be connected both ideologically and institutionally. Distrust and fear are particularly challenging obstacles. Some educational and community stakeholders may fear the lack of traditional structures and controls in these spaces. Others may express concern that utilizing community venues more intentionally will lead to the inevitable alteration or sanitization of inherently messy, organic spaces. What is unacceptable is to fail to reflect on, account for, and evaluate the influence of nonschooling venues, especially if discourses around equity, culturally relevant pedagogy, and closing achievement gaps are genuine. Regardless of one's apprehensions and inhibitions about the roles of learning spaces outside schools, the historical data remind us that these spaces represent a rich lineage of community-based education for people of African descent. To ignore the impact of these spaces is to ignore key cogs in the history, development, and sustenance of Black identities and Black cultures, and to ignore sites where education—irrespective of one's perception of its quality—takes place. Concomitantly, educational and community stakeholders act carelessly when they ignore how the organic nature of these community spaces can be both beneficial and detrimental, depending on who enters and leads these nonschool-based learning communities.

Our historical overview and our qualitative study data reveal that far less than thriving, some Black people are merely surviving, and too many others are being deprived of the necessary tools and opportunities (educational and otherwise) to challenge this reality. Sadly, the mantra "education by any means necessary" is often replaced by the bottom line: "survival by any means necessary." The lived experiences of the men in our oral history study suggest that much work still needs to be done to address the disproportionalities and disconnects that inhibit their capacity to cross literal and figurative borders. Although some of these men would describe themselves as successful, many of them have had to experience the bitter to know the sweet. Prison and other perilous circumstances have served as both tools of education and inhibitors to the fulfillment of big dreams.

What emerges from our study is the reality that community-based pedagogical spaces alone are not the panacea. In fact, the data reveal that there is no one space that meets the needs of every individual. Participation in community spaces is quite organic and fluid, as people go in and out of institutions and organizations. The implications of these realities for schoolhouse and nonschool-based outcomes are significant. Specifically, we are reminded that addressing one organization or entity will not allow us to address the needs of every student. Just like we must individualize instruction, an understanding of individual needs must undergird our approach to evaluating how spaces can be effectively utilized to buttress schoolhouse and other mainstream institutional approaches to education. Additionally, greater consideration must be given to the fact that education by any means necessary encompasses a range of processes and experiences that, at times, embody notions of survival, coping, deprivation, and thriving.

Conclusion

Through our study of history and our qualitative investigation, we conclude that it is important for all K–12 educational stakeholders (students, teachers, administrators, community members, policy makers, and researchers) to understand that education of Blacks has occurred and will continue to occur outside of schools. We believe there is potential for greater utilization of community-based pedagogical spaces to enhance the academic and life experiences of all students, and students of African descent in particular. In a time when policy makers are trying to address the overrepresentation of Black men in the penal system and scholar-practitioners are trying to close the achievement gap in schools between White students and students of color, this study offers an important reminder of the significance of alternative avenues in the educative experience. In this respect, our study challenges the orthodoxy that reforming schools, alone, will lead to greater academic success (Cuban 2010).

Our study is significant as a building block for future educative approaches that respect and incorporate the pedagogical potency of nonschool-based educational venues. For instance, scholars such as Franklin (1985), Seiler (2001), Mills (2005), and Hart and Bowen (2004), have considered the barbershop as a culturally relevant setting in the Black community for the study of topics ranging from Black male socialization practices to the dissemination of prostate cancer research. But little consideration has been given to partnerships that would foster pedagogical and institutional exchange and engagement between the barbershop and the K–12 schoolhouse (Douglas and Gause 2009). The barbershop could in fact be a possible site for early educational interventions intended to help youths navigate schools successfully (Author et al. 2009), even as we acknowledge that some messages and activities in these spaces may not always be positive (Franklin 1985; Harris-Lacewell and Mills 2004; Mills 2005).

In addition, as Gerald Horne notes in back cover praise of Swan's (2009) book, *Black Power in Bermuda: The Struggle for Decolonization*, there is a case to be made "for the importance of Bermuda as a laboratory for political developments that reverberated significantly on the U.S. mainland." Drawing on our previously stated belief that education must be more broadly defined to consider the impact of spaces outside of the schoolhouse, we believe that Bermuda can and must be used as "a laboratory" for greater understandings of Western educational constructs and their effects on peoples of African descent—peoples who are consistently required to cross literal and metaphorical borders to participate in the global community and the dominant Anglo-centered paradigms that are privileged in modern society. The privileging of the schoolhouse as the sole educative space for all young people and the inattention offered to learning spaces outside schools for Black people is emblematic of the cultural domination that must be considered if discussions of academic divides and achievement gaps are to evolve into more fruitful approaches and outcomes for all students. The findings of this study are our nascent efforts to participate in this process.

Although nonschool-educative venues like the Black church and the Black barbershop may be seen and described as nontraditional spaces in mainstream discourse and dominant schoolhouse settings, these spaces are actually traditional educative locale for peoples of African descent that continue to buttress and supplement the experiences that Black people have in the schoolhouse. Sadly, worse than being minimized as mere social or educational appendages, the power of nonschool-educative spaces to impact the educational experiences of Black youth has been virtually ignored or underutilized. This cannot continue. In the end, we believe that to help Black and other minority youth improve academically, school stakeholders must respect and show a willingness to embrace the culturally-grounded, educational traditions of African peoples. Specifically, we must pursue and achieve education by any means necessary.

Endnotes

1. Bermuda is often affectionately referred to as *The Rock* by many locals. Also, although Cyril Packwood's (1975) book, *Chained on the Rock: Slavery in Bermuda*, is not being directly referenced in this metaphor, it is significant to acknowledge his seminal work and the apparent, contemporary manifestations of Black Bermudian male oppression.
2. In Bermuda, discourses around race, achievement gaps, and schooling are often embedded in the overarching labels of public and private schooling, where the

majority of public school students are Black (Social and Demographic Division-Department of Statistics, Bermuda, 2006) and where most private schools are read as White, even though some Black students and other students of color attend these institutions (Christopher 2009; Douglas and Gause 2009).

References

Alim, H. Samy. 2011. "Global Ill-Literacies: Hip Hop Cultures, Youth Identities, and the Politics of Identity." *Review of Research on Education 35*: 120–146.

Anderson, James. 1988. *The Education of Blacks in the South, 1860–1935*. Chapel Hill, NC: University of North Carolina Press.

Anzaldua, Gloria. 2007. *Borderlands La Frontera: The New Mestiza* (3rd ed.). San Francisco, CA: Aunt Lute Books.

Bermuda Department of Statistics. 2006. *Characteristics of Bermuda's Families*. Hamilton, Bermuda: Bermuda Press.

Bernhard, Virginia. 1999. *Slaves and Slaveholders in Bermuda: 1616 – 1782*. Columbia, MO: University of Missouri Press.

Billingsley, Andrew. 1992. *Climbing Jacob's Ladder: The Enduring Legacy of African-American Families*. New York: Touchstone Books.

———. 1999. *Mighty Like a River: The Black Church and Social Reform*. New York: Oxford University Press.

Billingsley, Andrew and Cleopatra Caldwell. 1991. "The Church, the Family, and the School in the African American Community." *Journal of Negro Education* 60: 427–440.

Boogie Down Productions. 1990. *Edutainment* (Compact Disc). New York: Jive, B0000004WO.

Branch, Taylor. 1988. *Parting the Waters: America in the King Years, 1954–1963*. New York: Simon and Schuster.

Butler, Dale. 2006. *Triumph of the Spirit III*. Punta Gorda, FL: Atlantic Publishing House.

Carson, Clayborne. 1995. *In Struggle: SNCC and the Black Awakening of the 1960's*. Cambridge, MA: Harvard University Press.

Casey, Kathleen. 1993. *I Answer With My Life*. New York: Routledge.

Cassius, Samuel R. 1898. *Negro Evangelization and the Tohee Industrial School*. Reprint, Edward J. Robinson, *The Essential Writings of Samuel Robert Cassius*. Knoxville, TN: University of Tennessee Press.

Charters, Samuel Barclay. 2009. *A Language of Song: Journeys in the Musical World of the African Diaspora*. Durham, NC: Duke University Press.

Children's Defense Fund. 2007. *America's Cradle to Prison Pipeline: Summary Report*. Washington, DC: Author.

Christopher, Joseph. 2009. *A Random Walk Through the Forest: Reflections on the History of Education in Bermuda from the Middle of the 20th Century*. Winnipeg, Manitoba: Hignell's.

Cornelius, Janet. 1983. "We Slipped and Learned to Read: Slave Accounts of the Literacy Process, 1830–1865." *Phylon 44*: 171–186.

Cremin, Lawrence. 1970. *American Education: The Colonial Experience, 1607–1783*. New York: Harper and Row.

———. 1980. *American Education: The National Experience, 1783–1876*. New York: Harper and Row.

———. 1988. *American Education: The Metropolitan Experience, 1876–1980*. New York: Harper and Row.

Cuban, Larry. 2010. *As Good As It Gets: What School Reform Brought to Austin*. Cambridge, MA: Harvard University Press.

Dantley, Michael. 2005. "African American Spirituality and Cornell West's Notions of Prophetic Pragmatism: Restructuring Educational Leadership in American Urban Schools." *Educational Administration Quarterly*, 41: 651–674.

Douglas, Ty-Ron Michael O'Shea and Charles Phillip Gause. 2009. "Beacons of Light in Oceans of Darkness: Exploring Black Bermudian Masculinity." *Learning for Democracy 3*. Retrieved December 1, 2010. http://www.siue.edu/lfd/.

Douglas, Ty-Ron Michael O'Shea. 2012a. "Border Crossing Brothas': A Study of Black Bermudian Masculinity, Success, and the Role of Community-Based Pedagogical Spaces." Unpublished doctoral dissertation, The University of North Carolina at Greensboro.

———. 2012b. "Resisting Idol Worship at HBCUs: The Malignity of Materialism, Western Masculinity, and Spiritual Malefaction." *The Urban Review*, 44: 378–400.

———. 2013. "Confessions of a Border Crossing *Brotha*-scholar: Teaching Race With All of Me." Pp. 57–72 in *Social Justice and Racism in the College Classroom: Perspectives from Different Voices*. Edited by Dannielle Joy Davis and Patricia Boyer. Bingley, U.K.: Emerald Publishing Group Ltd.

Douglass, Frederick. 1995. *Narrative of the Life of Frederick Douglass*. New York: Dover.

Du Bois, William Edward Burghardt. 1973. *The Education of Black People: Ten Critiques, 1906–1960* (2nd Ed.). New York: Monthly Review Press.

Evans, Curtis J. 2008. *The Burden of Black Religion*. Oxford, England: Oxford University Press.

Fanon, Franz. 1963. *The Wretched of the Earth*. Translated by Richard Philcox. 2004. New York: Grove Press.

Fitzgerald, Rory, Steven Finch, and Andrea Nove. 2000. *Caribbean Young Men's Experiences of Education and Employment* (Research Report 186). London: DFEE.

Franklin, Clyde II. 1985. "The Black Male Urban Barbershop as a Sex-role Socialization Setting." *Sex Roles 12*: 965–979.

Freire, Paulo. 1993. *Pedagogy of the Oppressed: New Revised 20th-Anniversary Edition*. New York: Continuum.

Frey, Sylvia R. and Betty Wood. 1998. *Come Shouting to Zion: African-American Protestantism in the American South and British Caribbean to 1830*. Chapel Hill, NC: University of North Carolina Press.

Fultz, Michael. 1995. "African-American Teachers in the South, 1890–1940: Powerlessness and the Ironies of Expectations and Protest." *History of Education Quarterly*, 35: 401–422.

Gause, Charles Phillip. 2008. *Integration Matters: Navigating Identity, Culture, and Resistance*. New York: Peter Lang Publishing.

Gilborn, David and Heidi Safia Mirza. 2000. *Educational Inequality: Mapping Race, Class and Gender: A Synthesis of Evidence*. London: Ofsted.

Giroux, Henry A. 2005. *Border Crossings* (2nd Ed.). New York: Routledge Taylor & Francis Group.

Glesne, Corrine. 2006. *Becoming Qualitative Researchers: An Introduction* (3rd Ed.). Boston: Pearson.

Graham, Mekada and Gil Robinson. 2004. "The Silent Catastrophe: Institutional Racism in the British Educational System and the Underachievement of Black Boys." *Journal of Black Studies* 34: 653–671.

Hale, Janice E. 2001. *Learning While Black: Creating Educational Excellence for African American Children*. Baltimore, MD: Johns Hopkins University Press.

Harris-Lacewell, Melissa and Quincy T. Mills. "Truth and Soul: Black Talk in the Barbershop." Pp. 162–302 in *Barbershops, Bibles, and BET*. Edited by Melissa Harris-Lacewell. Princeton, NJ: Princeton University Press, 2004.

Hart, Alton Jr., and Deborah. J. Bowen. 2004. "The Feasibility of Partnering with African-American Barbershops to Provide Prostate Cancer Education." *Ethnicity and Disease* 14: 269–273.

Hicks, D. Emily. 1991. *Border Writing: The Multidimensional Text*. Minneapolis, MN: University of Minnesota Press.

Hill, Marc Lamont. 2009. *Beats, Rhymes, and Classroom Life: Hip-hop Pedagogy*. New York: Teachers College Press.

Hodgson, Eva Naomi. 2008. *The Experience of Racism in Bermuda and in its Wider Context*. Hamilton, Bermuda: Bermuda Press Limited.

Jones, Elizabeth. 1993. *Bermuda Recollections*. Hamilton, Bermuda: Globe Press Limited.

Jones, Major J. 1971. *Black Awareness: A Theology of Hope*. Nashville, TN: Abingdon Press.

Lincoln, C. Eric. 1989. "The Black Church and Black Self-Determination." Paper Presented at the Annual Meeting of the Association of Black Foundation Executives in Kansas City, Missouri, April.

Lincoln, C. Eric and Lawrence H. Mamiya. 1990. *The Black Church in the African American Experience*. Durham, NC: Duke University Press.

Lipsitz, George. 1994. *Dangerous Crossroads: Popular Music, Postmodernism, and the Poetics of Place*. New York: Verso.

Lovell, John, Jr. 1939. "The Social Implications of the Negro Spiritual." *Journal of Negro Education* 8: 634–643.

Manuel, Peter, Kenneth Bilby, and Michael Largey. 2006. *Caribbean Currents: Caribbean Music from Rumba to Reggae*. Philadelphia, PA: Temple University Press.

Margolick, David. 2000. *Strange Fruit: Billie Holiday, Café Society, and an Early Cry for Civil Rights*. Philadelphia, PA: Running Press.

Martin, Pamela and Harriette McAdoo. 2007. "Theological Orientation of African American Churches and Parents." Pp. 51–68 in *Black Families*, 4th ed. Edited by Harriette Pipes McAdoo. Thousand Oaks, CA: Sage.

McAdoo, Harriette Pipes. 2007. "Religion in African American families." Pp. 97–100 in *Black Families*. Edited by Harriette Pipes McAdoo, 4th ed., Thousand Oaks, CA: Sage.

Mills, Quincy T. 2005. "I've Got Something to Say: The Public Square, Public Discourse, and the Barbershop." *Radical History Review* 93: 192–199.

_____. 2006. "'Color-line' Barbers and the Emergence of a Black Counterpublic: A Social and Political History of Black Barbers and Barbershops, 1850–1970." Unpublished doctoral dissertation, University of Chicago.

Mincy, Ronald B., Monique Jethwani-Keyser, and Eva Haldane. 2009. *A Study of Employment, Earnings, and Educational Gaps Between Young Black Bermudian Males and Their Same-Age Peers*. New York: Columbia University School of Social Work; Center for Research on Fathers, Children and Family Well-Being.

Morrell, Ernest and Jeffrey Duncan-Andrade. 2002. "Promoting Academic Literacy with Urban Youth Through Engaging Hip-Hop Culture." *English Journal* 91: 88–92.

Morris, Jerome E. 2009. *Troubling the Waters: Fulfilling the Promise of Quality Public Schooling for Black Children*. New York: Teachers College Press.

Newton, Huey P. 1968. "The Correct Handling of a Revolution." *The Black Panther*, May 18.

Nunley, Vorris L. 2011. *Keepin' It Hushed: The Barbershop and African American Hush Harbor Rhetoric*. Detroit: Wayne State University Press.

Ogbu, John. 2007. "African American Education." Pp. 79–94 in *Black Families*, 4th ed. Edited by Harriette Pipes McAdoo. Sage: Thousand Oaks.

Packwood, Cyril. O. 1975. *Chained on the Rock: Slavery in Bermuda*. New York: Eliseo Torres and Sons.

Peck, Craig. 2001. "Educate to Liberate: The Black Panther Party and Political Education." Unpublished doctoral dissertation, Stanford University.

Perlstein, Daniel. 1990. "Teaching Freedom: SNCC and the Creation of the Mississippi Freedom Schools." *History of Education Quarterly* 30: 297–324.

_____. 2002. "Minds Stayed on Freedom: Politics and Pedagogy in the African-American Freedom Struggle." *American Educational Research Journal* 39: 249–277.

Putnam, Robert. 2000. *Bowling Alone: The Collapse and Revival of American Community*. New York: Simon and Schuster.

Runell, Marcella and Martha Diaz. 2007. *The Hip-Hop Education Guidebook Volume 1*. New York: Hip-Hop Association.

Seale, Bobby. 1991. *Seize the Time: The Story of the Black Panther Party and Huey P. Newton*. Baltimore, MD: Black Classic Press.

Seiler, Gale. 2001. "Reversing the 'Standard' Direction: Science Emerging from the Lives of African American Students." *Journal of Research in Science Teaching* 38: 1000–1014.

Sewell, Tony. 1997. *Black Masculinities and Schooling: How Black Boys Survive Modern Schooling*. Straffordshire, England: Trentham Books.

Shujaa, Mwalimu J. 1994. "Education and Schooling: You Can Have One Without the Other." Pp. 13–36 in *Too Much Schooling, Too Little Education: A Paradox of Black Life in White Societies*. Edited by Mwallimu J. Shujaa. Trenton, NJ: African World Press.

Stern, Richard G. 1961. "That Same Pain, That Same Pleasure: An Interview" in Ralph Ellison, 1964. *Shadow and Act*. New York: Random House.

Stovall, David. 2006. "We Can Relate: Hip-hop Culture, Critical Pedagogy, and the Secondary Classroom." *Urban Education* 41: 585–602.

Swan, Quito. 2009. *Black Power in Bermuda: The Struggle for Decolonization*. New York: Palgrave MacMillan.

Thompson, Paul. 1978. *The Voice of the Past: Oral history*. Oxford, England: Oxford University Press.

Turner, Sherry and Cherie Bagley. 2000. "The Role of the Black Church and Religion." Pp. 115–134 in *African American Woman: An Ecological Perspective*. Edited by Norma J. Burgess and Eurnestine Brown. New York: Falmer Press.

Tyack, David and Larry Cuban. 1995. *Tinkering Toward Utopia: A Century of Public School Reform*. Cambridge, MA: Harvard University Press.

Watters, Pat. December 20, 1964. "Their Text is a Civil Rights Primer." *The New York Times Sunday Magazine*, 10–11, 40–43.

Webber, Thomas. 1978. *Deep Like the Rivers*. New York: W. W. Norton.

Williams, Heather Andrea. 2005. *Self-Taught: African American Education in Slavery and Freedom*. Chapel Hill, NC: University of North Carolina Press.

Wilson, Camille M., Ty-Ron M. O. Douglas, and Christine Nganga. (in press). "Starting with African American Success: A Strengths-Based Approach to Transformative Educational Leadership." In *Handbook of Research on Educational Leadership for Diversity and Equity*. Edited by Linda. C. Tillman and James J. Scheurich. American Educational Research Association. New York: Taylor and Francis.

Wolff, Richard F. 1999. "A Phenomenological Study of In-church and Televised Worship." *Journal for the Scientific Study of Religion* 38: 219–235.

Woodson, Carter G. 1911. *Education of the Negro Prior to 1861*. New York: Knickerbocker Press.

———. 1932. "Is the Educated Negro a Liability?" *Chicago Defender*, May 21, A2.

Wrench, John and Edgar Hassan. 1996. *Ambition and Marginalisation: A Qualitative Study of Underachieving Young Men of Afro-Caribbean Origin.* London: Department for Education and Employment.

Wright, Richard. 1945. *Black Boy: A Record of Childhood and Youth.* Cleveland, OH: World Publishing.

Zuill, William. 1978. *The Story of Bermuda and Her People.* London: MacMillan.

Reading 7

A Conversation on the Literacy Development of Urban Poor Youth

Perspectives from the Classroom, Neighborhood and University

Ty-Ron M. O. Douglas, James F. Baumann, Adrian C. Clifton, Lenny Sánchez, Veda McClain, Pamela Ingram, and Ellis A. Ingram

> "Urban education" means something different to everyone based on their gender, race, sexual orientation, nationality, culture, socioeconomic status, age, or profession. In every definition, it is a juxtaposition of positive intentions and negative outcomes.
> (Kress 2006: 324)

Introduction

Although there is no dearth of research and theory on urban education (e.g., Khalifa, Dunbar, and Douglas 2013; Kincheloe et al. 2006; Pink and Noblit 2007), nor certainly on urban literacy education (e.g., Compton-Lilly 2012, Kinlock 2011; Lee 2007; Li 2007; Morrell 2007; Neuman and Celano 2012; Wilkson et al. 2008), there is little consensus on what it entails, as Kress (2006) notes (see above). What seems clear is that discourses and the harsh realities related to urban education in the US disproportionately affect students of colour, to the extent that little has changed since Kantor and Brenzel (1992) made this disturbing observation:

> After two and a half decades of federal, state and local efforts to improve urban education for low-income and minority children, achievement in inner-city schools continues to lag behind

Ty-Ron Douglas, James F. Baumann, Adrian C. Clifton, Lenny Sánchez, Veda McClain, Pamela Ingram, and Ellis A. Ingram, "A Conversation on the Literacy Development of Urban Poor Youth: Perspectives from the Classroom, Neighborhood and University," *Voices in Education: Journal of Bermuda College*, vol. 1, pp. 34-40. Copyright © 2015 by Bermuda College Journal. Reprinted with permission.

national norms and dropout rates in inner-city high schools (especially among African-American and Hispanic youth) remain distressingly high, while many of those who do graduate are often so poorly prepared they cannot compete successfully in the labor market. (p. 279)

In Bermuda, despite the reality that class-based borders and boundaries influence who occupies and has access to particular geographical and educational spaces (Douglas 2012a; Mincy et al. 2009), the language of urban space, urban education, or urban literacy education is far less common than in other countries and regions. Instead, particular neighbourhoods, locales, and school names have become polite—yet still problematic—indicators or labels of inequity.

Notwithstanding the growing body of scholarly research on Bermudian education in general, gaps remain. Scholars have certainly captured important elements of Bermudian history, culture, and education (Bernhard 1999; Burchall 2007; Butler 1987; Caines and Caines 2014; Christopher 2009; Douglas, in press; Douglas 2012a, 2012b; Douglas and Peck 2013; Hodgson 1997, 2008; Hunter 1993; Jackson 1991; Matthews 2003; Musson 1979; Packwood 1975; Robinson 1979; Swan 2009; Zuill 1999), but not necessarily explored the dynamics of literacy development in the context of Bermuda's unique cultural, social, and geographical constructs. We recognise, though, that attention to relationships between the nature of knowledge, identity, and race have been considered and cannot be absent from research in schools (Douglas and Peck 2013; Matthews 2003). In truth, this [reading] does not attempt to fill this gap, but our desire is to share and bridge an all-too-common conversation between educational stakeholders in Bermuda and the United States to spur on conversation about similar realities, challenges, and opportunities. As educators and scholars, one of whom attributes his academic and professional success to the sound educational experiences he had in Bermuda's public schools and Bermuda College, we recognise that we can no longer talk in silos about issues that are just as common in Columbia, Missouri as they are in Compton, California, and Cottage Hill, Hamilton Parish. Furthermore, continuing the rich legacy of Bermudian scholars who contribute to national and international conversations, this [reading] reveals how the voice of a Bermudian academician can be embedded in and enhance international discourses.

In this [reading], we address various complexities associated with teaching and supporting the literacy development of K-12 youth in urban poor school and community contexts. In so doing, it is our intent to address diverse conceptions of urban education, but more importantly, it is our hope that through an honest conversation about the vexing issues and questions facing teachers, students, and families who work and live in urban poor communities, our "positive intentions" and those of other literacy scholars can be (re)directed toward "positive outcomes" and success in schools and communities such as in Bermuda and the US.

The Structure

We seven coauthors are educators and community organisers with diverse backgrounds and experiences. We are collectively interested in enhancing the literacy development, life aspirations, and achievement opportunities for children and adolescents in urban poor school and community contexts. In this [reading], we draw on the concept of a Conversation Circle (CC) to raise questions and issues that intersect with our various contexts concerning urban literacy education. In a CC, participants convene in a circle, acknowledge one another as equals, invite inquiry, respect questions or confusion, suspend assumptions and certainty, are mindful of judgments, listen more than talk, accept the messiness of discourse, speak the truth from their experiences, and think together to create new knowledge (Rochte 2013). Rochte argues that CCs are much akin to an "elder's council, leadership circle, campfire circle, [or] roundtable" and that they are "embedded in our memes and maybe even our genes." In CCs "the question is more important than the 'answer'" (Rochte 2013: 1).

Drawing on this structure, we first center the voice of Ty-Ron Douglas by sharing a vignette that describes his selected personal experiences and concerns about literacy development. Next we include excerpts from an "open" CC dialogue that occurred with a public audience during a professional conference. We conclude with an appraisal of what we uncovered and is yet-to-be understood about promoting the literacy development of youth in urban poor settings through "the power of thinking together" (Rochte 2013).

A Personal Sharing

If the term "urban" were more common in Bermuda, it could be used to describe the neighbourhoods in which I, Ty-Ron Douglas, was reared. Growing up, my parents helped ensure I knew literacy mattered. To promote my literacy development, they purchased many books, National Geographic magazines, and a word of the day calendar. I read few of the books, occasionally scanned pictures in the magazines, and learned one word from the calendar, "facetious." Undoubtedly, my parents' influence was important but insufficient in my literacy development. In truth, school and community-based educators helped buttress my development in this regard. I remember the day my affinity for words was sealed: it was the afternoon I unleashed "facetious," in context, on my unsuspecting Primary 3 teacher (Ms Rochelle Furbert) as she sought to reprimand me for talking too much. Rather than punish me, Ms Furbert inquired if I knew how to spell and define the word. I certainly did, gladly taking the opportunity to display my vocabulary skills in front of my classmates. She then affirmed me for my mastery of a word above my grade level, which buoyed my confidence and left a distinct impression upon my literacy development.

Other community-based pedagogical educators impacted my journey and literacy development (Douglas 2014; Douglas and Peck 2013). One such educator was my barber, Ricky Spence. For over 30 years, Ricky's Barbershop has served as a hub—a classroom—for working class Black males for fellowship, sharing and learning. Ricky promotes literacy by purchasing the daily newspaper for his patrons to read and discuss. He has facilitated the literacy and educational development of thousands of Black males by moderating robust, culturally relevant barbershop dialogue that is often instigated by the print and digital media materials he makes available. Certainly, my career and commitment to literacy development and leadership have been shaped by educators like Ricky and Ms Furbert. We would do well to recognise and maximise the pedagogues and pedagogy of leaders in spaces inside and outside the traditional schoolhouse (Douglas 2014; Douglas and Peck 2013).

The Conversation

Building on this vignette in what follows, we highlight three themes we believe are important for augmenting our understandings of literacy development for educators of urban youth across various locales: overcoming barriers to learning, transformative engagement and moving towards action. These themes emerged from a cross-narrative analysis of the topical impulses that developed from a face-to-face dialogue with the other educators at the 63rd Literary Research Association Conference who joined us in question-posing, experience-sharing and problem-solving centered on the topic of literacy in the urban context. Some of their voices are recognised in the following sections by the name "Conversation Member."

Overcoming Barriers to Learning

A question from Ms Ingram: How do we negotiate cultural and environmental barriers to learning—such as family dysfunction, community violence, fatherlessness, poverty, abuse, incarceration—that some children bring into the classroom to enable them to actually "hear" and learn?

Dr McClain: We must do so gingerly and respectfully. Our urban poor cut across racial and cultural lines, and what has become more apparent over the past few years is that many families do not know how to stop the generational dysfunctions that prohibit and inhibit learning for their children. Parents at my school have begun to seek assistance from the school so they can learn what they need to do as parents to promote academic success. We share strategies and activities they can use at home with their children as well as ways to interact more positively with teachers.

Ms Clifton: It is necessary to address the issues Pamela notes both inside and outside schools? I also challenge pre-service and in-service teachers to volunteer in their students' communities. They must be a light in the darkness and a part of the village that raises a child.

Conversation Member: As Ms Ingram suggests, we must establish permanence with our children and families so they can rely on us. They wonder: "Are you going to be there tomorrow? When I turn 12? At Christmas?"

Dr Ingram: I have found this to be so very true with our outreach programmes. When a person volunteers or provides service outside the classroom, the families are watching very closely to find out how long you will be there. It probably took us a few years to gain that confidence from our students and their families.

Dr Douglas: I think we must carefully analyse how we see young people. We must beware of deficit-based approaches that position students, their neighbourhoods, and their culture as half-empty. Certainly, family dysfunction, community violence, fatherlessness, poverty, abuse, and incarceration are real. Still, using an anti-deficit lens, I wonder how we can (re)frame these challenges as pedagogical infrastructure so the process of "hearing" and learning can be more reciprocal between the children, teachers, and leaders.

Dr Sanchez: Teachers certainly play a tremendous part in this process. A good friend of mine serves as the principal of an alternative high school. At this school, teacher meetings consist of check-points where they can share struggles and successes, as well as opportunities to enter into conversations about what it means to be a compassionate, respectful, truthful, and responsible teacher. She provides them multiple opportunities through course design and co-teaching, for example, where they can nurture personal passions so these interests seep into the energy of students' learning.

Dr Baumann: Our discussion makes me think of the large-scale studies conducted in the 1970s and 1980s on what was called "teacher effectiveness." That research demonstrated that successful teaching and learning occurred in classrooms in which teachers had high expectations, believed in students' abilities, and had a confident, optimistic "can-do" attitude. I believe that David Berliner used the word convivial to describe these environments. The research also demonstrated that effective teachers had a sense of humour, provided praise and communicated to children a sincere sense of caring—these were happy classrooms where students felt secure and valued.

Ms Clifton: Yes, we must be there with encouragement, a smile, and a hug—understanding that outside the school walls is where the real war is taking place.

Transformative Engagement

A question from Dr Sanchez: How can literacy be used to affirm and reflect students' lives? When do literacy practices and pedagogies promote or prevent children and youth from transformatively engaging with their world?

Dr Sanchez: We know that literacy is tied to social and economic opportunity and that it should not be taken lightly. Literacy is, after all, a regulation of access to particular subjects, forms, and ideas; and schools can either work to maintain or disrupt the advantage of these purposes. For literacy to affirm and reflect students' lives, teaching and learning must value students' experiences, desires, wonderings, and needs so that those become what is important in the classroom. This means we cannot let standards or prescribed curriculum take away the skills and knowledge students have.

Conversation Member: I have been a teacher in schools identified as "urban" or "serving diverse populations" and have invested in social justice and critical pedagogy. I believe in acknowledging, affirming, and building on students' literacy practices and the texts they use and generate at school, in their homes, and around their communities.

Dr Sanchez: Jabari Mahiri (2004) uses the term "street scripts" to describe the kinds of texts students produce, perform, and publish in their everyday interactions. Examples include video, rap, spoken word, art-making, and any type of written or spoken language fashioned to express or expose daily experiences. In Valerie Kinlock's (2011) book, *Urban Literacies*, teacher educators, researchers, and scholars share similar ideas for how students can use pop culture, digital media and other forms of multimodality to fine-tune literacy skills that also promote varied ways of researching their communities. What all of these concepts have in common is that literacy instruction becomes transformative for a student when teaching and learning are rooted in the students' sociocultural and historical understandings of themselves and their communities. The goal for the teacher is to work towards utilising instructional designs of agency that encourage students to be creative, innovative and responsive to their needs and those they learn about.

Moving Towards Action

A question from Ms Clifton: How do we move towards action when confronted with research that shows our urban children as failing and after conversations like these, where the issues are highlighted even more?

Dr McClain: One action is to engage and partner with parents in helping them to understand the varied literacies children need to be successful in schools and in pursuits after schooling.

Conversation Member: I think that action largely depends on hope. I recall a powerful presentation at AERA by Sean Ginwright, who suggested that present-day children of poverty lack hope. When we can help instill a sense of hope, many changes are possible.

Dr Ingram: This is so true. It is so important to help students think through their own challenges and set goals based upon expectations set by themselves and others. I sincerely believe there is a unique brilliance in each and every student: we need to help them see it.

Dr Douglas: I agree, but we don't need to just move towards action; instead, we need to engage in reflective, thoughtful action. It's a cyclical process, where reflective action is partnered with critical reflection and strategic collaboration with other stakeholders.

Dr Baumann: This discussion reminds me of the qualities of teacher researchers, who possess an insider, or emic, view of teaching and learning, and who mix theory and practice, or praxis. Cochran-Smith and Lytle (1999) argued that we must find a way to add a critical dimension in which teachers move "between their classrooms and school life as they struggle to make their daily work connect to larger movements for equity and social change" (p. 291).

Ms Clifton: For me, I move towards action by waking up each morning and taking personal responsibility to walk what I talk.

Afterword

What can we conclude from our CC and "the power of thinking together"? We recognise that each of us has different experiences, different perspectives, and different points of view on the literacy development of urban poor youth. That is neither surprising nor unfavourable, although at first blush this may not seem like "thinking together." Yet we do see commonality in our beliefs and convictions reflected in our conversation. Across the spectrum of our conversation, we see potential in our three cross-cutting themes (overcoming barriers to learning, transformative engagement, and moving towards action) and want to make clear they are undergirded by anti-deficit conceptualisations of literacy development for urban youth. We believe any solution to educational reform or dilemma must "sing the praises" of youth and honour their linguistic, cultural, and intellectual resources. This means literacy teaching and learning must invoke the virtuosity of youth while taking into consideration any political and cultural ideologies connected to the students' schooling context that may be rooted in prejudice or stereotype. Said another way, there is a need to build on and create bridges between the background knowledge and skill-sets urban poor youth bring to the classroom and the new knowledge and skills educators seek to impart.

In regard to broadening how pre-service teachers see and experience urban space, we ask university education programmes to consider how they might broaden the scope of their curriculum to include dimensions of community attachment. This includes service opportunities, but also examining the social and political capital of a particular community. The goal of this type of work would be to understand what it takes to significantly alter the life chances of an individual from a low-resourced community. We know communities have the capacity to change the conditions impacting their members. Pre-service teachers, in-service teachers, and teacher educators alike must look within communities to examine how community citizenship, for example, is promoted and encouraged and determine ways to make the schooling curriculum responsive to a community's needs.

Lastly, to reiterate our CC, we recognise there is an ongoing need to (re)evaluate our motives, expectations, and methods towards the instigation of a socially just movement that will lead to more equitable opportunities and outcomes for urban poor youth. While student success in Bermuda or the United States is grounded in our willingness as educators to better understand the unique context of the geopolitical and educational urban terrain in our jurisdictions, we cannot lose sight of the larger regional, national, and global discourses that unify us as pedagogues and leaders. Rather than working to write a single story of what it means to teach "urban poor youth" across (inter)national and (sub)urban borders, our students often have much in common, despite their diverse needs. Our responsibility is to not only engage in conversations with and about similarities and differences, but to then work to find culturally relevant solutions to our localised and global educational challenges that can necessitate change beyond the borders that most closely surround us.

References

Bernhard, V. (1999) *Slaves and slaveholders in Bermuda: 1616–1782.* Columbia MO: University of Missouri Press.

Burchall, L. (2007) *Fine as wine: From coloured boy to Bermudian man.* Chapel Hill NC: Professional Press.

Butler, D. (1987) *Dr. E.F. Gordon: Hero of Bermuda's working class.* Bermuda: The Writer's Machine.

Caines, W.M., and D.A. Caines (2014) *Double vision: A journey to success.* Capshaw AL: Spirit Reign Publishing

Christopher, J.T. (2009) *A random walk through the forest: Reflections on the history of education in Bermuda from the middle of the 20th century.* Winnipeg: Hignell's Book Printing.

Cochran-Smith, M. and S. Lytle (1999) The teacher research movement: A decade later. *Educational Researcher* 28(7): 15–25.

Compton-Lilly, C. (2012) Reading time: *The literate lives of urban secondary students and their families.* New York: Teachers College Press.

Douglas, T.M.O. (in press) Exposure in and out of school: A Black Bermudian male's successful educational journey. Teachers College Record.

Douglas, T.M.O. (2014) Conflicting Messages, Complex Leadership: A Critical Examination of the Influence of Sports Clubs and Neighborhoods in Leading Black Bermudian Males. *Planning and Changing* 45(3/4): 311–38.

Douglas, T.M.O. (2012a) Border crossing brothas': A study of Black Bermudian masculinity, success, and the role of community-based pedagogical spaces. (Unpublished doctoral dissertation, University of North Carolina at Greensboro NC).

Douglas, T.M.O. (2012b) Resisting idol worship at HBCUs: The malignity of materialism, Western masculinity, and spiritual malefaction. *The Urban Review* 44(3): 378–400.

Douglas, T.M.O. and C.M. Peck (2013) Education by any means necessary: An historical exploration of community-based pedagogical spaces for peoples of African descent. *Educational Studies* 49(1): 67–91.

Hodgson, E. N. (1997) *Second-class citizens, first-class men* (3rd ed.) Canada: The Writer's Machine.

Hodgson, E.N. (2008) *The experience of racism in Bermuda and in its wider context.* Bermuda: Bermuda Press.

Hunter, B.H. (1993) *The people of Bermuda: Beyond the crossroads.* Toronto: Gagne-Best.

Jackson, W.V. (1991) *The Jackson clan: The story of a Bermudian family.* Bermuda: Bermuda Press.

Kantor, H. and B. Brenzel (1992) Urban education and the "truly disadvantaged": The historical roots of the contemporary crisis, 1945–1990. *Teachers College Record* 94(2): 278–314.

Khalifa, M., C. Dunbar and T.M.O. Douglas (2013) Derrick Bell, CRT and educational leadership 1995-present. *Race, Ethnicity, and Education* 16(4): 489–513.

Kincheloe, J.L., K. Hayes, K. Rose and P.M. Anderson (eds) (2006) *Praeger handbook of urban education*. Westport CT: Greenwood Publishing.

Kinlock V. (2011) Urban literacies: *Critical perspectives on language, learning, and community*. New York: Teacher's College Press.

Kress, T. (2006) Purple leaves and charley horses: The dichotomous definition of urban education. In J.L. Kincheloe, K. Haynes, K. Rose and P.H. Anderson (eds) *The Praeger handbook of urban education* (Vol. 1) (pp. 324–9). Westport CT: Greenwood Publishing.

Lee, C. (2007) *Culture, literacy, and learning: Taking bloom in the midst of the whirlwind*. New York: Teachers College Press.

Li, G. (2007) *Culturally contested literacies: America's "rainbow underclass" and urban schools*. New York: Routledge.

Mahiri, J. (ed.) (2004) *What they don't learn in school: Literacy in the lives of urban youth*. New York: Peter Lang.

Matthews, L.E. (2003) Babies overboard! The complexities of incorporating culturally relevant teaching into mathematics instruction. *Educational Studies in Mathematics* 53(1): 61–82.

Mincy, R.B., M. Jethwani-Keyser and E. Haldane (2009) A study of employment, earnings, and educational gaps between young Black Bermudian males and their same-age peers. New Columbia University School of Social Work, Centre for Research on Fathers, Children and Family Well-Being.

Morrell, E. (2007) *Critical literacy and urban youth: Pedagogies of access, dissent, and liberation*. New York: Teachers College Press.

Musson, N. (1979) *Mind the onion seed*. Bermuda: Island Press.

Neuman, S.B. and D.C. Celano (2012) *Giving our children a fighting chance: Poverty, literacy, and the development of information capital*. New York: Teachers College Press.

Packwood, C.O. (1975) *Chained on the rock*. Bermuda: Island Press.

Pink, W.T. and G.W. Noblit (eds) (2007) *International handbook of urban education*. Dordrecht, The Netherlands: Springer.

Robinson, K.E. (1979) *Heritage*. New York: MacMillan Educational.

Roche, M. (2013) The natural way humans think together. Retrieved on 01/15/14 from http://conversationcircle.com

Swan, Q. (2009) *Black power in Bermuda: The struggle for decolonisation*. New York: Palgrave MacMillan.

Wilkinson, L.C., L.M. Morrow and V. Chou (eds) (2008) *Improving literacy achievement in urban schools: Critical elements in teacher preparation*. Newark DE: International Reading Association.

Zuill, W.S. (1999) *The story of Bermuda and her people* (2nd ed.). London: MacMillan.

CPSIA information can be obtained
at www.ICGtesting.com
Printed in the USA
BVHW052309120920
588366BV00004B/260

9 781516 594962